★ ★ ★ PRAISE FOR ★ ★ ★
GUNNY'S RULES

"Read and heed! My friend R. Lee Ermey has packed a pithy bio and a lifetime of 'Corps values' into *Gunny's Rules*. The only people who won't love this book are thumb-sucking, tree-hugging, belly-crawling maggots."

—**LT. COL. OLIVER NORTH**, USMC (Ret.),
author of the *New York Times* bestseller *Heroes Proved*

"In his typical gritty and courageous way, The Gunny pulls no punches in this true-to-life rendering of some of life's greatest lessons. *Gunny's Rules* is a must-read not only for U.S. Marines but for everyone interested in getting a no-nonsense guide to some of life's toughest lessons."

—**MAJ. GEN. J. A. KESSLER**, USMC (Ret.)

"Having known The Gunny for many years as a fellow Marine and a fellow showbiz professional, I can affirm that what you get in this straight-shooting, hard-hitting new book is the real deal. R. Lee has given us all-important insights coupled with solid doses of commonsense wisdom in this work. Whether or not you feel the need to get squared away, you'll be glad you read this book. Bravo Zulu, Gunny!"

—**CAPT. DALE DYE**, USMC (Ret.), founder of Warriors, Inc. and
technical advisor on *Saving Private Ryan* and *Band of Brothers*

"Gunny tells it like it is! I read a lot of leadership books, most of which are written by people who have read other leadership books and want to add their version but know nothing about leadership! Gunny speaks from real-world experience. This should be mandatory reading for every NCO and Staff NCO in the Marine Corps."

—**GENE OVERSTREET**, USMC (Ret.),
Twelfth Sergeant Major of the Marine Corps

"I thoroughly enjoyed this read. The behind-the-scenes look into the filming of *Full Metal Jacket* and Lee's relationship with Stanley Kubrick was interesting. More important, though, those who know and appreciate what Lee has done are likely to view his rules for life as an honest assessment of what people look for in achieving some level of success. Those who have served will relate; those who have not will understand. Lee's honest appraisal of his own shortcomings as a youngster and what kind of determination it took to get a leg up on the rest is a valuable lesson for anyone looking to become successful."

—**MIKE KESSLER**, national director and CEO of
Young Marines of the Marine Corps League

"The Gunny's done it again! Real, raw, and revealing, R. Lee weaves his amazing life into a must-read how-to lesson for life. The Gunny is a true American original, and now he's written a playbook for anyone who wants to live the true American dream."

—**ROE CONN**, talk radio host of *Roe & Roeper*, WLS-AM 890 in Chicago

"R. Lee Ermey, aka 'The Gunny,' has given us a quick, most enjoyable read about his experiences growing up, his lessons learned serving in the Marines, and his most successful career as both a talented actor and a successful businessman. Everyone in our Corps of Marines understands that the Non-Commissioned Officers are the backbone of our Corps. This little book will help you understand why! *Gunny's Rules* and the various related quotations are priceless and most applicable for all as they go through life."

—**GEN. AL GRAY**, Twenty-Ninth Commandant, USMC (Ret.),
senior fellow and chairman of the Board of
Regents of the Potomac Institute for Policy Studies

"The most original self-help book ever—great fun to read and truly inspirational!"

—**SIDNEY J. FURIE**, director, *The Boys in Company C*

★GUNNY'S
RULES★★★

GUNNY'S RULES

HOW TO GET SQUARED AWAY LIKE A MARINE

R. LEE ERMEY

REGNERY
Publishing, Inc.
An Eagle Publishing Company • Washington, DC

Cataloging-in-Publication data on file with the Library of Congress

ISBN 978-1-62157-159-9

Published in the United States by
Regnery Publishing, Inc.
One Massachusetts Avenue NW
Washington, DC 20001
www.Regnery.com

Published in association with
MacGregor Literary, Inc. of Hillsboro, OR
Represented by Sandra Bishop

Written with Lamar Underwood, who diligently helped
the author get his voice on the page.

Manufactured in the United States of America

10 9 8 7 6 5 4 3 2 1

Books are available in quantity for promotional or premium use. Write to Director of Special Sales, Regnery Publishing, Inc., One Massachusetts Avenue NW, Washington, DC 20001, for information on discounts and terms, or call (202) 216-0600.

Distributed to the trade by
Perseus Distribution
250 West 57th Street
New York, NY 10107

*This book goes out to all who have served our country,
especially my brother and sister Marines who've stood in the yellow footprints.*

*Also, God bless the six most influential people in my life:
my three Marine Corps Drill Instructors and Sidney J. Furie, Leon Vitali, and
Stanley Kubrick.*

CONTENTS

"If you're not fifteen minutes early, YOU'RE LATE."

—R. Lee Ermey, a.k.a. The Gunny

FOREWORD

IT'S GOOD TO KNOW THE GUNNY

L eo Durocher once said that "nice guys finish last," but after working as R. Lee Ermey's personal manager for over twenty years—with nothing more than a handshake agreement between us—I gotta say, I take issue with that particular generalization.

I'm sure you picked up this book hoping to learn more about what made The Gunny who he is. Of course certain characteristics define a person. But, I assure you, there is more to the man than the hard-ass most people see in the movies or on TV.

The Gunny does quite a few personal appearances throughout the year on behalf of the various companies he proudly represents at trade shows and major retail outlets. There are always long lines of people patiently waiting an average of three hours to meet him and get his autograph. He truly is a rock star in these environments. When people meet him, he looks them in the eye—not because he's attempting to intimidate, but because he's genuinely interested in connecting with people in a meaningful manner. He goes out of his way to pose for pictures, engage in conversation, and make every effort to individually connect with as many folks as he possibly can.

Whether it's on the street or at a personal appearance, The Gunny treats people with respect and affection. Unlike any other celebrity I know, he spends a fair amount of quality time with each and every individual he meets, doing his best to make sure they enjoy an experience with him, not just a casual meeting. He doesn't just *meet* their expectations, he exceeds them.

Honestly, it's quite a powerful thing to witness his fans walk away with smiles on their faces. I've been with him at high-profile events where other agents and managers walk their clients over and point him out, saying, "Look, this is how you need to be with people. See how he makes everyone feel special! Why can't you do that?"

Some might think the way he engages with folks is a talent he has cultivated over time, or that it's just good PR, but I know better. He's simply the most genuine, hardest-working man you'll ever meet.

One day, The Gunny woke up and fell out of bed. Something definitely was not right, but he wasn't about to miss work, or let down his crew, so he walked around, shook it off, and got himself to the set in Santa Clarita, California, where we were filming his long-running History Channel show, *Mail Call*. As the day wore on, he began occasionally slurring his speech and dragging his left leg. Obviously we were very worried, so the on-set medic checked him out and tested him for a stroke and other potential symptom-related maladies.

He didn't find anything, but I tried anyway to get him to go to the hospital right then and there. The Gunny strong-armed us all and kept insisting he was fine, just a little tired. He couldn't be swayed, but we agreed to a compromise. I made sure he made an appointment to see his personal doctor the next morning, and he worked the rest of the day like the Marine that he is.

Later that night, however, his daughter called to tell me she was taking him to the hospital because he had a pounding headache that wouldn't go away. The doctor did a CAT scan and casually asked him if he had recently hit his head. He thought for a moment and remembered an incident that happened two months before, while filming a scene for his wicked role in *The Texas Chainsaw Massacre* in which an actor had to jump him from behind and smash his head against the ground. He was in the moment, worrying about whether it appeared real, and was more concerned with whether they'd gotten the shot than he was about his own well-being. Apparently, as the doctor explained, this had caused a subdural hematoma due to a micro-leak from a blood vessel in his brain.

For two months, blood had been slowly pooling behind his skull. When it had nowhere else to go, it finally started to press inward on his brain, which resulted in the stroke-like symptoms that we had witnessed on the *Mail Call* set. Of course they immediately took him to surgery, where they cut out a piece of his skull, drained out about a coffee cup full of blood, and repaired the leak. Once the swelling went down, they replaced the skull fragment and put multiple staples in his head to close the wound. Two days after this final procedure, he tried to convince the doctors that he was able to go home, jumped out of bed, and promptly fell on his ass.

A couple of days later, he was finally able to convince his doctor to let him go home for bed rest. However, as soon as he got home, he took a shower, packed his bag, and headed out to Camp Pendleton for a previously scheduled personal appearance that he had no intention of missing. I couldn't be there, but I hear he gave one helluva motivational speech—head staples and all! Which didn't surprise me in the least, because that's just the type of guy he is.

It's a challenge to work for The Gunny and not sound like a walking commercial for the man, knowing firsthand that he donates about one hundred days per year to causes and events. Nothing gets in the way of his charitable, military, and law enforcement obligations.

Over the years, The Gunny has turned down numerous lucrative film and television roles that happened to conflict with one of these commitments. This kind of thing drives other agents and managers crazy, but I've always understood it. That's The Gunny.

The Gunny visits our wounded warriors in military hospitals whenever he gets the chance. It's very humbling to watch him during these encounters. I often find myself looking into the faces of vets who have made such huge sacrifices on behalf of our country, and I witness something I don't think he recognizes. When they see The Gunny from their hospital beds as he walks into their rooms, their eyes light up, almost as if they're innocent six-year-olds again, meeting Santa Claus at the mall. Make no mistake, he knows his purpose is to cheer them up, brighten their day, salute them, and pay his respects for their sacrifice. He is keenly aware of how they perceive him and of the impact he makes on them. But I think there is more to these hospital visits than a sense of personal duty. I'm fairly certain that the biggest impact of these visits is on The Gunny himself. I truly don't know how he can stay so strong and upbeat in the face of such tremendous suffering.

On the sixtieth anniversary of D-Day, we were in Normandy filming a special *Mail Call* episode. At one point as the sun was setting, we found ourselves alone in the Normandy American Cemetery and Memorial, long after it had closed for the day. Every single member of our film crew was unable to control his or her emotions when faced with the overwhelming casualties and gravity of the scene. While we rode silently back to our lodgings, each of us trying not to look at one another for fear the tears were still contagious, I noticed The Gunny was certainly not immune.

The Gunny takes tremendous pride in the companies and products he represents as a spokesperson because he truly believes they're the best. He won't work with a company he doesn't believe in. Whether he's adding to his motorcycle collection or knife collection, buying some clothing and gear, or looking for a new firearm, he genuinely appreciates and values the gear they send his way to test, use, and abuse. Only the best earn the right to be called Gunny Approved™. He's as real a guy as you'll ever meet and has a lot of fun with the gear and perks he receives, but he certainly doesn't take any of the privileges of his spokesperson gigs, or his celebrity, for granted.

During Operation Iraqi Freedom, our History Channel *Mail Call* production crew was filming *Mail Call: Live from Iraq*. While there, we were filming at Ali Al Salem Air Base in Kuwait, twenty-three miles south of the Iraq border, and we happened to be staying in a five-star hotel that the History Channel had booked for us. We had a large crew, and because we had booked so many rooms, they gave the host of our show, The Gunny, the 1,500-square-foot Presidential Suite. It was opulent, to say the least.

The morning after our first night, he phoned my room, completely pissed off. "Billy, I ordered eggs, toast, and coffee, and it came to $50!" he said. I explained that the History Channel knew where they'd put us up and told him they certainly knew what things cost there—and not to worry about it; the History Channel was paying the tab. He told me he didn't care who was paying for it, it still "chapped his ass" to unnecessarily spend that kind of money, whether it was his money or someone else's. And that was the last I heard about it, or so I thought.

The next day, The Gunny called me to his suite to join him for lunch, where I found him sitting on the floor eating an MRE (Meals Ready to Eat). I asked him what he was doing, and he told me that he'd be eating MREs for the rest of the trip—the same food our troops were eating. He proceeded to show me a case of various MREs that he had gotten from our U.S. troops at the base. We ate an MRE lunch together, and he continued to extol the virtues of the MRE. "If it's good enough for them, it's good enough for us." We stayed at that hotel for a full week, and he managed to keep the total cost of his hotel meals under $100!

After the show had aired live in the States, our sweltering stay in Kuwait, and the palatial hotel, was over. When we were getting ready to head to the airport, The Gunny informed me that he'd decided to stay behind an extra week in order to visit our troops at small outposts throughout some of the most dangerous parts of Iraq. I tried to convince him that the Marines couldn't *guarantee* his safety and that the History Channel would be none too pleased. He told me, "Billy, our troops don't need another celebrity visiting them in *the rear with the gear*. Quit your worrying. Do you think my Marines are going to let anything happen to me?"

He donned a flak jacket and a helmet, hopped on a helicopter, didn't shower for a week, and puddle-jumped from place to place— visiting the troops in areas of Iraq that never *ever* got any celebrity visitors.

The Gunny, host of their highest-rated series, couldn't have cared less what the History Channel might have thought about it. He's always been about morale-building, and he had troops to visit. Yep. Just the type of guy he is.

In 2009, *USA Today* ran a feature about The Gunny, plucked from the AP:

> Actor R. Lee Ermey is living up to the Marine Corps' mantra: "A Few Good Men."
>
> The former Marine Drill Instructor and host of The History Channel's *Mail Call* was in Missoula[, Montana] on Monday to film a segment for his television series, [*Lock N' Load with R. Lee Ermey*,] when he said he found some cash. A lot of cash.
>
> Ermey, best known for playing Gunnery Sergeant Hartman in Stanley Kubrick's *Full Metal Jacket,* said he was driving with crewmember Harlan Glenn to a museum when he spotted a black object on the road.
>
> Ermey stopped the car and picked up the bag, which contained cash and checks that looked like they were meant for deposit in a Native American fund.

"Just on one deposit slip alone was, like, $3,700, and another one for $2,800," Glenn said. "There was easily $8,000 in cash and the rest in checks."

Ermey told the Missoulian newspaper he thought: "Some poor guy right now is probably getting fired, probably having the worst day of his life. So what we did was we went right down to the Wells Fargo bank and deposited it for him."

Don Luke, a business expert at the Wells Fargo branch, said he was surprised to see "The Gunny" stroll in.

If I had been there, I wouldn't have been surprised at all. Because, you guessed it, that's just who he is.

I'm excited that *Gunny's Rules* will finally give readers a window into the qualities of the man I have long considered a good friend. Although we do not always share the same politics, we do share the same ideals. What you are about to read is a collection of moments and events that have defined and shaped R. Lee Ermey into the man I know so well. He is almost twenty years my senior, yet he is more like a brother to me than a client. He doesn't have a prejudiced bone in his body, and he respects everyone's right to exist and enjoy what our wonderful country has to offer. "To each his own, Billy," he often says to me. "Who am I to judge?" A pretty good policy, if I say so myself, and one that I have personally worked hard to emulate.

Something else he likes to say is, "It's good to be The Gunny."

I happen to believe it's also very good to *know* The Gunny. He's living proof, and hope for all of us, that nice guys don't always finish last.

—Bill Rogin, personal manager/producer/director,
Rogin Entertainment, Beverly Hills, California

INTRODUCTION

GETTING SQUARED AWAY

In my more than fifty years of serving the Marine Corps, and my nearly forty years as an actor, I think I've learned a few things, and I feel it's time to pass them along. That's the reason for this book. I think there's something in it for everyone from age fourteen to 104, though I should give fair warning that the language might be occasionally salty—but only when necessary, because that's the way it was.

If you're reading this book, you probably know me well enough to know that I don't mince words, gild lilies, or play politically correct games. If you want it straight, damn straight, you'll get it here.

I know—from the messages I've received from viewers of my *Mail Call* television series, from conversations I've had with folks at trade shows, and from discussions with countless Marine brothers and sisters—that a lot of you want to know more about my experience making a film, *Full Metal Jacket*, that has become an American icon.

(And, yes, dammit, I'm allowed to say that about my own movie—because it's true!)

The making of *Full Metal Jacket* was a learning experience for me second only to Marine Corps boot camp. In fact, when I relive my experiences filming the movie *Full Metal Jacket*, it almost seems like another duty station.

If you want to know more about my experience in that movie, you're not going to be disappointed. I intend to take you behind the scenes on the film that gave R. Lee Ermey's career a boost far beyond any possible expectations. By the way, *Full Metal Jacket* was film number five out of more than seventy!

But this book is not solely or even primarily about *Full Metal Jacket*. Throughout the course of this book, I intend to take you to other movie sets and through my life in the Marine Corps in a way that I hope you will find useful and illuminating. My goal is to show you some of the rules I've learned, some of the rules I live by, some of the rules that I think might benefit you the reader if you'd like to get your life squared away.

"Squared away" is an honorable and venerable expression that's a Marine Corps favorite and has also become part of modern language in general. Literally, it means that everything is shipshape, organized, fine-tuned, and ready to go. Its origin is sometimes traced all the way back to the great clipper ships having their topsails square to the wind. Sometimes it is traced to another aspect of the United States Navy—as when sailors try to get their white, circular, Dixie Cup–looking hats—"covers" in Marine language—adjusted to just the right angle. In any case, "squared away" is the condition you want: ready to pass inspection from life's Drill Instructors, ready to succeed and lead. So if you're ready, let's go!

—R. Lee Ermey

CHAPTER

"FALL IN!"

TAKE COMMAND OF YOUR LIFE

The deeply rutted trace of a road I had been following into the mountains suddenly grew wider as it climbed steeply through a pine thicket. There were hard-edged ruts all over the place. Some wise-ass had painted a sign and nailed it to a tree beside the trail. It read: "Choose your rut with care. You'll be in it for the next 10 miles."

He knew a thing or two, the guy who had tacked up that warning—about backcountry roads anyway.

So did I.

My experiences with ruts had started many years before I read that sign. I knew all about them. And I knew that the ruts in real life are like the ones in the road—hard to escape.

The ruts in your life can hold you for months and years, just like the miles. The next ten, the next twenty...on and on.

I've hit my share over the years—and managed to tear myself free from them all.

You can do the same.

Like a director calling "Action!" to start a movie scene, I'm calling you loud and clear to make hard decisions, jump-start new goals—and square your sorry butt away!

T he brim of the Smokey Bear cover worn by the Marine Drill Instructor was locked against my forehead, burning like a steel blade. His mouth was only inches from my face, and the screams emerging were commands from hell: "Who dressed you this morning, Scumbag? Your daddy? I saw you talking after we told you to shut up and line up. Do that again and I'll gouge your eyeballs out and skull-fuck you, you little shit."

On the outside, I was trying to stand tall on the yellow footprints painted on the pavement at the receiving barracks of the Marine Corps Recruit Depot in San Diego, California. But inside I was trembling, unable to flee, and barely able to withstand the ordeal I was facing. Coming here was a big mistake. I had really screwed the pooch this time. I was wishing I could go back home to our family's farm near Toppenish, in Washington state.

> **"You know damned well you can't go back home. Go back, and you'll go to jail."**

"You know damned well you can't go back home," my thoughts screamed. "Go back, and you'll go to jail."

The Drill Instructor's tirade went on without interruption. As the minutes crawled by, he never once repeated himself, and I never stopped cringing in my gut.

Along with a bunch of other recruits, I had just scrambled from the cattle car, a six-by truck set up like a bus to haul recruits to the depot. The Drill Instructor onboard had shouted, "Get rid of the gum! Cut the chatter! You've got one damn minute to get off the bus and position your useless selves on my yellow footprints. Go! Move it! Move it!"

Everybody had lunged for the doorway and the footprints where we were to line up. Suddenly, we heard a new command. "Hold it up, you people! You're too freaking slow. Get back on the bus."

We had to get back on the bus to go through this ridiculous bullshit five or six times because some jerk in front was taking his sweet-ass time. Before we'd even learned to stand at attention, some of us were learning to police our own ranks. I told the guy in front of me, "Listen here, asshole. You better get your butt in gear." And then a Drill Instructor cried, "Who's that talking over there?" And suddenly I was caught in the DI's crosshairs. He had to make a statement, right at the receiving barracks door. He had chosen me to make an example with.

Now there I stood at the receiving end of this DI who was yelling X-rated obscenities, stuff I couldn't imagine in a thousand nightmares. He even said nasty things about my family!

It was the third of April 1961. I had just turned seventeen a couple of weeks before.

Hard to believe, but I had intended this to be my salvation, my escape from the difficult life I had left behind. My goal, my mission, seemed destined to fail now. And I had no backup plan.

Finally there came the moment when I began to realize that my father's intense and frequent ass-chewings back on the farm had hardened me for the verbal whiplash I was now facing. The difference was that the Marine DIs were strangers and professionals, masters of the greatest motivators, pain and intimidation. They could verbally chastise you like nobody else on earth. Still, they were only screaming. There was spittle, but nobody had hit me yet.

Hell, I had lived through this on the farm, why not here?

Suddenly, I began to feel myself digging in. They couldn't get rid of me by screaming at me.

Two weeks before, I had not been a happy camper. For sure, I hadn't even been a camper.

Campers have fun, roasting marshmallows and weenies beside crackling fires and hiking trails to adventure. There was no fun and no adventure in the farm field where I was trying to wrestle a stinking, creosote-soaked fence post into the stubborn ground. My wiry 139-pound body hurt like I was being punished. Perhaps I was. I was a high school dropout at tenth grade, with a juvenile delinquency record on the books—a farm boy with seemingly no future but the farm.

At that age, I was not given to reflecting on the pleasant sides of farm life—hunting opportunities, enjoying nature, things like that. With my five brothers, a caring mother, and an irascible father, I was a veteran of hard-core farmland living, having already spent most of my young life on a spread in the remote Kansas croplands. Our place in Washington State, where we lived when I was older, was different in many ways, but the chores and work were about the same. Take, for example, the fence post I was fighting right then. Under the demanding, critical eyes of my father, I was hacking out my third hole of the day for that one post. The other two had been "a little out of line."

I didn't know what an "event horizon" was back then. When I thought of horizons, I had visions of palm trees, Hula girls, and tropical paradises, but my real horizon looked pretty barren. Days filled with chores like hefting backbreaking hundred-pound bales of alfalfa, milking cows, splitting wood, and shoveling manure in summer and snow in winter. And planting creosote posts.

Thank God I was smart enough to realize that life didn't owe me a living—it didn't owe me a damn thing. Still, I believed there had to be something better in life for R. Lee Ermey. I had to get moving!

The law helped. In the City Hall of Toppenish, Washington (population about eight thousand back then), a judge had given me a choice: go into the service, or I was headed for a place where the sun didn't shine. That wasn't just a nudge. It was a shove that sent me straight into the Navy recruiting office right there in the building. I confess I wasn't very surprised when they told me to hit the road. They didn't want me.

As I walked slowly down the hall, boards of the wooden floor creaking as I pondered what I was going to do now, I approached a life-sized cardboard recruiting poster of a Marine standing tall and proud in his dress blue uniform.

The image held me. My gaze stayed locked on the splendid figure of a man who looked very fit, proud, and even happy. This farm boy knew nothing about the Marine Corps, but I figured that anybody who wore a fancy uniform like that, with a white belt, a white hat, and white gloves…well, it was obvious he didn't have to work very hard. I should look into this.

Could this be my chance? I opened the nearby door and stepped inside.

The recruiter was sitting with his feet on the desk, reading a copy of *Mad* magazine. He took his feet off the desk, closed his magazine, and laid it aside. "Well, young man," he said. "What can I do for you?"

I told him I wanted to join up.

He looked at me and pointed to the door. "Jump up on that door sill right there, and let's see how many pull-ups you can do."

I liked the sound of that. Farm work had made me wiry and strong despite my light weight. I grabbed the sill and began doing pull-ups. As I passed fifteen, starting to feel the pain, I wondered if twenty was the magic number the recruiter wanted. No matter. At eighteen I was all the way out.

I dropped to the floor, arms aching. Would eighteen be good enough?

Then I heard the sweetest sound that had ever come to my young ears: "Outstanding. You're hired!"

Now, at the yellow footprints, the three Drill Instructors were doing their thing. They tore into our group, screaming and jumping up and down. They were all red faced, blood vessels swelling in their necks, their eyeballs bulging out. It was ugly and scary. The expression "shock and awe" would not come along until the war in Iraq, but I can see now, looking back, that I was experiencing it then, full bore.

The Drill Instructors knew what they were doing, of course. They were not training men to teach Bible school. We were being taught to kill for God, country, and the Corps.

During my first week of the twelve-week recruit training, my goals began coming clear. I kept telling myself: I will grow, I will exercise, I will become strong. I will listen to my Drill Instructors. They will teach me to do close-order drill, they will teach me the rifle manual and marksmanship, they will teach me pugil sticks and bayonet fighting. They will teach me to be aggressive. And that's what I need to be. Then I will graduate. Then I will be a Marine. And I will be proud.

Recruit training is the same today, as tough as it can be, because it still works, just as it worked with this skinny maggot in 1961. I made it through boot camp and became a Marine—ready, willing, and able to eat my own guts, and willing to advance on, engage, and destroy the enemies of my country.

But let's fast-forward eleven years to 1972, when I stood wearing civilian garb on the curb beside my seabag, outside the gate of the Marine Corps' Air Station at Cherry Point, North Carolina. Behind me, on board the Marine bases where I had been posted, were the only friends I had ever known. Behind me were all the challenges and experiences I had ever loved.

The Marine Corps had retired me, and retirement had caught me by surprise. I had expected to be a Marine for the rest of my life.

But there would be no more Halls of Montezuma, no more shores of Tripoli for Staff Sergeant R. Lee Ermey.

A rocket attack on the Marine side of Da Nang Air Base in Vietnam a couple of years before had sealed my fate. We'd taken eight or nine rocket hits that night, and one of them sent a heavy bunker timber crashing down on my shoulder, dislocating it. I walked to the sick bay and stayed a while, but they were so busy with badly hurt, bleeding Marines that I went on back to my unit, where I'd had a whiskey before my fellow Staff NCOs twisted and pulled my shoulder back into place. In the months that followed, it would never stay. Any surprising, sudden jerk of my arm would cause that shoulder to pop back out of joint.

My original objective had been to stay in the Marine Corps for a full thirty years and attain the rank of Sergeant Major. And my ultimate goal was to become *the* Sergeant Major of the Marine Corps.

The Navy doctors had other ideas. The Vietnam War was winding down, and the Marine Corps troop numbers with it. Anyone not one hundred percent, top-notch, physically fit would have to go. Because I had been in for more than ten years, they couldn't just discharge me. But they could, and did, put me out on medical retirement. So now I get a very small *tax-free* check every month. Don't tell the IRS.

Standing at the curb outside the Cherry Point Marine Base in North Carolina, on the "yellow footprints" of civilian life, I felt many of the same emotions of uncertainty and fear that had been with me back on day one of my Marine life. Once again it was "guts-up" time. All I knew was that I would be bunking with a former Marine buddy in the Los Angeles area for a while. I needed to look for a job, but I knew not what or where.

I was starting over. Square one. Age: Twenty-eight. Qualifications: To be determined.

As things turned out, I found a job. Then another, then another. I moved around a lot and tried a lot of different things. All the while, I kept reaching, hoping, and trying to do better.

Some would say I was lucky.

Sure, I had some good breaks. But to me, they were just well-timed opportunities.

The motion picture business is tough to crack into, but the Marine Corps had taught me the true meaning of professionalism, and it was easy to outshine the undisciplined civilians in Hollywood. A walk in the park. I wanted to give it a try. So, when a chance to be hired came my way, I was ready to take full advantage of the good fortune.

The years that followed put me on the sets of seventy-five feature films and made-for-television movies and 114 episodes of my television shows, *Mail Call* and *Lock N' Load with R. Lee Ermey*. Some amazingly talented people gave me the opportunities to use my abilities in works audiences appreciated.

But that was not enough.

Yes, I was in movies and working on television. I was making good money. To many people, I was considered famous. What more in God's name could I possibly want?

I wanted to continue serving my country as a Marine.

I wasn't the retired, "Once a Marine, always a Marine" type. I wanted to literally continue as a Marine. I wanted to find a way to continue my association with the Corps and stand beside my brother

The Marine Corps had retired me, but I kept showing up for work.

and sister Marines whenever and wherever possible. No, I couldn't go on patrols in the jungle with six canteens strapped to my web belt the way I had done on active duty. I couldn't be a BAR man, lugging a Browning Automatic Rifle, or a squad leader, or a Drill Instructor at a recruit depot. But I was determined to serve my beloved Corps through activities devoted to its history, its personnel, and its future.

The Marine Corps had retired me, but I kept showing up for work.

My celebrity helped me to serve my beloved Corps in a unique way, and I was present for duty every chance I could get, whether as a guest speaker at Marine Corps Birthday Balls in Japan, Okinawa, Guam, and Gitmo; on appearances on bases with the troops; on the silver screen, showing them respect in my television shows; or visiting troops in Iraq and Afghanistan. I was out there at every opportunity, doing what I could to boost the troops' motivation and morale.

That's my job as a Marine Staff NCO, which I still am and always will be. *Ooorah!*

Eventually, in 2002, Marine Corps Commandant General James Jones bestowed an unexpected honor and gesture of respect upon me for my continued support of the Corps. The General promoted me to Gunnery Sergeant, making me the only Marine ever promoted after being retired. The ceremony took place at the Marine Corps Recruit Depot in San Diego. This is my home away from home, the place where my Marine adventures started. Since I live in California now, the Depot and nearby Camp Pendleton are frequent destinations where I regularly hang out with the troops and stay up on what's happening.

My promotion to "The Gunny" meant that my activities with the Marine Corps would become more intense than ever, visiting troops at Marine Corps bases and "outside the wire" at outposts in Afghanistan and Iraq. As The Gunny, I could get more done with Marine Corps charities and get the word out on the hard jobs Marines were doing all over the world. As The Gunny, my television shows and appearances would have more impact, more personality.

I felt reborn as a Marine, and it has been one hell of a motivator for me—not that I ever lacked motivation.

Though I play one in the popular Geico commercial, I'm not really a psychiatrist. Nor am I a natural philosopher or learned professor. I feel blessed, however, by experiences that have taught me enduring lessons about taking command of my life.

We all know there are no guarantees in life. But don't let that stop you. I never did. I've always loved stepping up to the plate. That's the part I like best about my roles in life: taking a good swing at the ball, sometimes striking out, sometimes knocking it over the fence. Win, lose, or draw—it's always another adventure.

Yes, I had a rough start, but—and I say this with all humility— if I could live life all over again and I were given the opportunity to be anybody else, I would still want to be me. It's good to be The Gunny!

What if you don't like your life or the way it's going? Whose fault is that? You've got the means to pull yourself out of whatever ruts you're in instead of just letting them take you where they will. It will take effort, but when you get your wheels up over the hump and start heading toward a destination of your choosing, you'll be amazed at how your life can change.

Your Gunny has no commands, no marching orders for you. But I do offer some observations, alerts, and tips that seem worth sharing after years of gleaning them from my experiences working in the world of filmmaking, enjoying the great outdoors, living with friends and family, and, of course, serving in the United States Marine Corps.

Throughout my journey, I have tried to hold onto lessons learned from all the low and high points—especially the lows, for it is those times when we're knocked onto the deck that we build the strength that helps us get back up and carry on. Life is as good as you make it.

Not everything I have to say will fit your personal situation. But I'm betting you'll find more than a few things here that will stick—things that will help you over the hump, help you get up the hill, and maybe even help you out of your own ruts.

Since I've already confessed to not being a philosopher, you'll understand my leaning on one of the best, a certain Mr. Johann Wolfgang von Goethe, who lived back in the eighteenth and nineteenth centuries. Among other things, he said:

Whatever you can do,

Or dream you can,

Begin it.

Boldness has genius, power

And magic in it.

You can tack that one on the bulkhead of your memory. I especially like the phrase, "Or dream you can...."

I can make that shot. I can climb that mountain. I can swim that river. I can land that new job.

I can take responsibility for changing my life for the better.

Still with me?

You'd better be! Or you'll miss out on some straight talk on making your life worth living and getting your future squared away.

GUNNY'S RULES FOR
TAKING COMMAND

★ IT STARTS WITH A PAYCHECK

For me, getting and holding a job has always been goal one in civilian life. No matter what job I was holding, I was always looking for a better one. But I never turned in my two weeks' notice until I had landed the new job. For a time, I became the master of the two weeks' notice, jumping ship often and fast. But I was never without a job or income.

I'm a proud man, not a dependent. I will still be providing for my family long after I'm dead and gone. Unemployment checks, welfare, and food stamps won't cut it, in my view. They're like quicksand, sucking you under. There may come a time when you can never get out. You drown.

That's a hell of a shame, because I firmly believe you can accomplish any reasonable goal that other human beings all around you are taking on every day. A job as a short-order cook is a hell of a lot better than sitting on your dead ass watching television all day. With that job comes self-respect, the kind of self-respect that can lead to new goals. It won't be easy, but as your pride grows, so will your reach. You'll see goals worth fighting for. If they're not worth working and fighting for, they're probably not worth having.

> **A job as a short-order cook is a hell of a lot better than sitting on your dead ass watching television all day.**

★ SET REASONABLE GOALS, NOT MOON SHOTS

You need to be reasonable about setting your goals. Remember that you need to walk before you can run—and *then* you can pick up the pace.

I've always been a goal-setter, and I've always been so reasonable with my goals that when I achieve what I'm after, I quickly find myself saying I have to set new, higher goals.

Always work on new goals while you keep those paychecks coming. Unless you're about to inherit Aunt Millie's fortune, it's the only way to find the happiness we all seek. Forget about the lottery, Vegas is not going to happen, and I doubt you'll strike oil in your backyard. Work, work, work…work! Earn it, Jack!

★ ADJUST YOUR TARGET

Goals can shift. They're subject to revision, fresh opportunities, and fresh thinking. One of my five brothers offers a good example of this.

Like all of my other brothers, he spent time in the service. When he left the Marines after four years, he entered barber school. There's nothing on earth wrong with that. But when the opportunity to join the telephone company came along, he grabbed it. He knew he would have to study hard and work hard, and he knew he would be challenged. But he was willing to take a chance and was confident he'd succeed. And he did. He has enjoyed a wonderful career and lives in a beautiful, mountainous area of California. Perhaps he would have been just as happy as a barber, but I don't think so. As it is, I've got the best of all possible worlds—a brother with a great career at the phone company and a great house in the mountains who's always willing to cut my hair.

✪ CONFIDENCE: THE LINCHPIN OF SUCCESS

When you're ready to attack a new goal, you need to be ready, prepared, and confident—and the most important thing is confidence. If you're not confident you'll succeed, you never will.

When I was very young, before I went into the Marine Corps, my loss of confidence almost destroyed my life. Here's how it happened:

I grew up on a farm eighteen miles west of Kansas City, Kansas, where the Speedway is now.

My mother and we boys ran the farm for our own support. A sign down our long lane alerted passersby that we had chickens, eggs, and milk for sale at the house.

I was number two of six boys, so when I was seven or eight, it was up to my older brother and me to handle the chores—milking and haying cows (sometimes using a sledgehammer to break ice on the pond so the cattle could drink during the winter), mending fences, feeding chickens, gathering eggs, and helping our mother clean and dress the chickens for sale. For extra money I worked on neighboring farms.

In addition to our own livestock, the hunting in the area was terrific, with plenty of pheasants, rabbits, and ducks. The school bus stop was a mile away, and I carried my shotgun with me in the morning, stashing it in a culvert along with any game I had shot on my way to the bus stop, then picked it back up after school and hunted my way back home.

School through the sixth grade was in a two-room building, with the first, second, and third grades in one room, and the fourth, fifth, and sixth in the other. There were six rows of desks with ten farm kids in each row. That's sixty kids to two teachers. Kinda blows away the sorry excuse that our kids can't read because of overcrowded classrooms. Maybe there's another reason, because I can damned sure read!

My schooling, or its shortcomings, caught up with me, though.

We moved to Washington state, where my dad's uncle was a contractor who owned a farm with acres of Concord grapes leased to Welch's. He gave my dad a job, a generous move.

School was a different story in Washington. The kids in my class were so far ahead that I could never catch up. I should have been put back a grade, but it didn't happen. I struggled and struggled, trying to do the work my classmates were doing. They left me in the dust.

My ego and confidence were totally destroyed. I remember the overwhelming sense of failure draining every tiny bit of confidence I had ever known. I fell in with the wrong group of boys, losers like me. With them, I got into trouble. You know what happened next, how the Marine Corps became my redeemer.

If you lack confidence, things get ugly. Everybody around you is setting off to climb the mountain, run the river. You're slumping to the side, saying, "You guys go ahead. I'm not ready."

You've got to convince yourself you are capable. It's all about you! Nobody else. It's about dedication, applying yourself, and doing whatever it takes to make it happen—studying, working out, and even seeking help if need be.

That new job you want, that lean and fit body you wish were yours—they're not going to come knocking on your door, looking for you.

You've got to build a game plan to go after those goals. And once you go in to attack, make confidence and determination your leading weapons.

★ DO IT FIRST, TALK ABOUT IT LATER

If you're young and trying to take on new goals for yourself, you have to beware letting your buddies hold you back with their dumb-shit attitudes. If they haven't got the message that life is about goals and work, then the hell with 'em. Don't let them trip you up. You've got things to do and places to go. Dump the losers! Just get the hell away from 'em!

For young people who are still dependents, living at home, unless your household is completely screwed up, you probably should discuss your plans with your parents—perhaps at the supper table. Hell, they might even be able to help.

Other than talking with parents, I would recommend holding your cards pretty close to your shirt. Just because you have friends doesn't mean you have to tell them all your hopes, dreams, and plans. Sometimes jealousy and negativity of certain friends can be destructive, especially in today's flow of information over the internet. I wouldn't want to read about somebody pissing all over my plans on Facebook, especially plans they had no business knowing about to start with.

I'm at the point today where I don't tell anybody but Mrs. Gunny and my agent about my plans for the future. I wait until I've accomplished the mission or I'm at the point where success is assured.

Doing it first, talking about it later is usually the way to go. It works for me. No one gets in my way!

★ THE BIG LIFE DECISION: YOUNG MARRIAGE?

Taking command of your life includes the big decision to get married. As a husband, you need to be ready to take command, with all that entails. And you have to be ready to take orders as well as give them. Every husband knows that "Yes, dear" is the marital equivalent of the military "Yes, sir."

Some young folks are ready for that—they're ready to take command. So I'm not dead set against young marriage. I'm not especially for it, either.

Marriage, done right, is one of the greatest ways of getting squared away. The trick is, you have to be squared away before you do it.

Having your sweetheart become your lifetime partner will only work out if you're both established in your personalities, education, and employment goals.

All over the world, pilots of big jets, from Lufthansa to American Airlines, share a common check on their takeoff roll. They call out, "Power set...stable engines."

If your young marriage does not have "power set" and "stable engines," you're going to crash and burn. You probably won't even get off the runway.

You can prevent that by considering that you must come to your marriage with a solid and satisfactory way of making a living to pay the bills. You need to be in a job you like. (That doesn't stop you from looking for a better one, of course.) Your education...well, if you're cutting it short, you must realize that you're going to have to live with that decision and its consequences. (Did you copy that? There *will* be consequences.) Your personalities...the dipshit kid stuff has to be over.

Okay, you've got a job at the gas station or beauty shop. You think your future looks good, and you're dying to marry your sweetheart. Try to remember what I'm saying about being stabilized, capable, and willing to pitch in for what's meant to be the long haul. It's almost impossible to pursue a career and raise a family at the same time—you can't give one hundred percent to either.

There's a lot of pick-and-shovel work to be done to keep a marriage squared away, whether you're young or mature. The old joke that a husband or wife is your "ball and chain" is true. You're never on your own anymore. What's good for one has to be good for the other. Of course, there's a romantic side to your marriage as well, and that's pretty important, especially for her; she needs to know, and you need to know—and abide by this—that you love her and have, as the marriage vows go, forsaken all others. You're with her for life: till death do you part. The rewards, you don't need to remind me, can be immense. My wife (she likes to be called "Mrs. Gunny") and I have been married for over thirty-five years.

So there you go, young lady, young man, with some straight talk for your coconut to get a grip on before you say, "I do." Make success come first, then marriage.

TAKING COMMAND
QUOTES WORTH REPEATING

"Man's greatest unhappiness comes from giving up what he wants most for what he wants now."

—Anonymous

"The life you have led doesn't need to be the only life you'll have."

—Anna Quindlen

"Flipping burgers is not beneath your dignity. Your grandparents had a different word for burger flipping...they called it opportunity."

—Bill Gates

"The secret of getting ahead is getting started."

—Mark Twain

"To recognize that the greatest error is not to have tried and failed, but that in trying, we did not give it our best effort."

—Gene Kranz, Apollo 13 flight controller

"In any moment of decision, the best thing you can do is the right thing, the next best thing is the wrong thing, and the worst thing you can do is nothing."

—Theodore Roosevelt

"You miss one hundred percent of the shots you never take."

—Wayne Gretzky

"Do not let what you cannot do interfere with what you can do."

—Coach John Wooden

"Laziness travels so slowly that poverty soon overtakes him."

—Benjamin Franklin

"The greatest discovery of my generation is that a human being can alter his life by altering his attitude."

—William James

"We must take the current where it serves, Or lose our ventures."

—William Shakespeare, *Julius Caesar*

"The only place 'success' comes before 'work' is in the dictionary."

—Vince Lombardi Jr.

"Hitch your wagon to a star."

—Ralph Waldo Emerson

"If you are going through hell, keep going."

—Winston Churchill

"Excellence is the result of caring more than others think is wise, risking more than others think is safe, dreaming more than others think is practical, and expecting more than others think is possible."

—Anonymous

CHAPTER

"BE PREPARED"

THE BOY SCOUTS GOT IT RIGHT!

You've heard that 80 percent of success in life is just showing up. When I show up, you can count on my being prepared to win!

My future was far from being squared away when I bunked on my buddy's couch in L.A. for a couple of months after being medically retired. It was a time of uncertainty as I took on odd jobs, trying to bring my goals into focus. One of the things I remember most fondly about that time was the skit I started doing in comedy clubs. These weren't big-time deals; sometimes there were only four or five people in the audience. It was more like karaoke is today. I got up there and launched into a Drill Instructor routine. People loved it, and I loved doing it, even though I did not have a clue where it would lead. There were damn sure no hecklers, and when one did have the guts to challenge me, it added a lot of entertainment value. But they soon regretted it.

After a short time in L.A., my drifting came to an end.

I was single, looking for adventure. I was also looking to become a big success. I had made up my mind that a person had to own his own business to really cash in—had to be his own boss, call his own shots. But not in L.A. If I was going to attack a new endeavor, I needed some level of familiarity and certainty in my arsenal.

I packed my seabag, drove over to George Air Force Base in San Bernardino, jumped on a space-available flight, and never looked back. As far as I know, my old car is still sitting there in the Base Operations parking lot.

My view out the window of the plane was of the vast Pacific Ocean. I was on my way toward a new adventure. Destination: Kadena Air Force Base, Okinawa, Japan.

To the Japanese, the island of Okinawa is like Hawaii is to Americans—a tropical paradise. It has beautiful weather and palm trees all surrounded by an ocean of crystal-clear green water. I still think it's the most beautiful water in the world. Of all the duty stations on which I served during my eleven years in the Marine Corps, this was the one I appreciated the most. It was also the last overseas station I served at before the Corps retired me. And I had a few girlfriends there.

Now I was coming back, with money in my pocket and a $350 monthly retirement check I could count on. I was good to go. Hell, I had all the confidence in the world that I could live really well there while finding my way to fame and fortune.

The Marine Corps has always maintained a strong presence on Okinawa, and that was still very much the case when I returned there as a civilian. I wanted to be near the base at Camp Hansen, where I knew most of the senior Staff NCOs. Because the Marine Corps is a relatively small organization, one of the best ways you get to know everyone at any base is by meeting for lunch at the Staff NCO Club, which is what I started doing the minute I got back. Walking into the club was a great experience, seeing who was there, then seeing old buddies come in the door. They were always interesting—hard-core war fighters who had been in Korea and Vietnam, or even in World War II. There were Marines there who had been at Tarawa and Iwo, on the frozen retreat from the Chosin Reservoir in Korea, and at the long siege of Khe Sanh. Their stories were fascinating, but none of them lived in the past. They loved the here and now. The area also had a lot of retired Marines, called "Far East Bastards." Many had married Okinawan or Japanese girls.

> **I knew that with just a little preparation, I could run the best damned bar ever.**

The plan for my next move was hatched right there. It occurred to me that the type of business most familiar to me from all my years as a Marine was the bar business. And I knew that with just a little preparation, I could run the best damned bar ever.

After about a month, I found an empty bar I could lease in Kin Village, a small village just outside the Camp Hansen main gate, which provided easy access to the services Marines needed most: female companionship, restaurants, bars, tailor shops, pawn shops. The place I found to lease had a bar, a fridge, and tables and chairs scattered on the deck. That was it. No stock—booze—had been left behind.

After setting up my lease, my wallet was thinner than I ever hoped to see. I had just enough dough to buy one bottle of each popular type of liquor—bourbon, vodka, gin—plus a few bottles of the most popular choice of Marines—scotch. There was no keg beer on Okinawa then, except on the base, so I bought one case of Orion beer and stashed it in the fridge, along with some Cokes and drink mixers. I was opening on a shoestring, but I was opening.

I spread the word about the bar at the Staff NCO Club, and just as I hoped they would, the Marines landed in full force. As the cash came in, instead of going into the till, it went into the waiting hands of my girl Friday, who ran off to buy more booze, beer, and ice. We operated that way for a couple of nights. Then the till swelled to an operational size, and the place was off and running. There was no stopping this Devil Dog now.

With money pouring in, I was able to get some help and open the bar in the mornings, at zero seven thirty. We were the only place open at that time of day. I served coffee and made sure I had plenty of copies of *Stars and Stripes* waiting for our customers. Someone tended the place every day at noon when I went back over to the Staff NCO Club to spread my bar's matchbooks on the tables, talk up the place, and buy lunch for some of the guys. They had a lot of freedom back then, in '73 and '74. The Staff NCOs called the shots and ran the Corps. If they wanted to take an afternoon off, so be it. I never left the Staff Club without three or four SNCOs tagging along.

The bar was called "Beer House Bear," simply because that was the name on the sign out front and I never changed it. I couldn't afford to, at first, and I didn't want to later. We became so popular that sometimes we would have one hundred patrons packed in the place at one time. Since we didn't have a kitchen, there was no food, but I did make pickled eggs available at a buck each, and we sold jarfuls of them every night. I made them myself, every week or so, a nasty job.

One of the reasons for our success was the comedy routine I had experimented with back in the L.A. comedy clubs. I sometimes did my Drill Instructor gig there in my own bar, and the troops ate it up.

After about eight months or so, I found a bigger place, a hotel, and bought the joint. It needed to be fixed up, but the Marines at base maintenance took care of that for me. They arrived in six-bys loaded with plywood, saws, paint, hammers and other tools. They were carpenters, plumbers, painters, and maintenance guys in their own right who knew what they were doing. In two days they gutted the existing first floor and turned the place into a bar that was to die for. The only thing it cost me was free beer. We called the place the "SADA": Sunday Afternoon Drinking Association.

For four years I lived in the goal I had achieved. I'd wanted my own business and to be my own boss. I had attained that. I suppose I could have decided that I was set for life.

But I didn't. I was restless, still. As Okinawa had come more and more under Japanese jurisdiction, I could feel life changing in ways I did not personally appreciate.

Right about the time I began wondering about a new goal, a new challenge, it walked into the front door of my bar.

Over his drink, a Marine said, "Hey, Lee. I've heard that Hollywood people are gearing up in the Philippines to make movies about Vietnam."

A game changer had arrived, and I was prepared. The next day I started looking for a buyer for the bar.

Eventually, I found myself back out at Kadena Air Force Base, asking to hitch another space-available ride—this time to Manila in the Philippines.

I was still single, and I still had a check coming in every month, but now I had a seabag filled with money I'd earned from the bar. I was ready to move on, take new chances, and do bigger and better things. The airman behind the desk told me there was a C-130 on the ramp right then, warming up to go to Clark Air Force Base in the Philippines. I could make it if I hurried.

Could I ever! I hustled my butt and seabag of money onto the plane and settled down to think about what might lie ahead. While I looked out the window of the plane into the same sea over which I'd flown to my last adventure, I realized I was really only sure of one thing: If there was a tiny crack in the movie business door, I was going through it. I would succeed no matter what!

Despite the rumors, the movie people had not shown up in full force when I got to the Philippines. I stayed in Manila for about two months, hanging out, looking for contacts. Then, in my usual style of looking to make some money while I was waiting for movie action, I moved to Cavite, a little town on the coast, about two hours north of Manila. I bought a forty-foot fishing boat, hooked up with a crew who knew how to run it and catch fish, and just like that, I was in the fishing business.

I divided my time between fishing and making the rounds where movie contacts might be found. I talked with everybody who might help me. I did some schmoozing, buying drinks and dinners. I learned that there was only one American casting director in the entire Philippine Islands. His name was Ken Metcalfe. I found him, and right away we hit it off. That led to having drinks together many times, then dinners. I even bailed him out of jail once. Hell of a guy!

You might say he owed me. Whether he did or not, he came through for me.

The first film to get cranked up in all of the new Philippine moviemaking activity was *Apocalypse Now*, directed by the already-legendary Francis Ford Coppola of *The Godfather* fame. Ken Metcalfe arranged for me to meet Coppola. Our conversation was short; Coppola was a very busy man. He turned me over to the number one technical advisor, and I was in. He hired me for the job of number two technical advisor for *Apocalypse Now*.

> **I found Ken Metcalfe, and right away we hit it off. I even bailed him out of jail once. Hell of a guy!**

Now my foot was firmly wedged in that door to the movie business I had been thinking about when I left Okinawa. I let the fishing crew have the boat, just turning it over to them, and immersed myself in my duties. I basked in the challenges of filmmaking and my surroundings. Every day was an adventure, a learning experience. Then, two months into the filming, disaster struck.

A typhoon roared through the Philippines, taking lives and destroying homes and property. It made shambles of our sets for *Apocalypse Now*. The production had to be shut down. It looked like my start in the movie business was already over.

Not quite. Coppola kept us on retainer while he returned to the States to raise more money for the production, which was only half filmed at this point.

Now, instead of being put out of business, I had a new opportunity. I had a retainer check, my monthly retirement check, and money in the bank. While *Apocalypse Now* was shut down, I had the chance to look around and see what the other movie people were doing—a chance to kick tires, talk to people, make stuff happen.

Once again, Ken Metcalfe paved the way for me. He introduced me to Sidney J. Furie, a director who had come to the Philippines to scout locations for shooting a movie called *The Boys in Company C*. Furie, a Canadian by birth, was a very experienced director with a solid background of credits. I met him in his office with his secretary and a couple of assistants.

Furie seemed likeable, a fellow I could get along with very easily. Right away he asked me if I could call cadence.

Was he kidding, or what?

I asked him if he wanted to close the door, because this was going to be sort of loud.

He said it wasn't necessary.

I boomed out a couple of cadences, my voice shaking the walls.

"You're hired!" Furie said.

I was slated to become technical advisor for *The Boys in Company C* when the filmmaking got underway. If things worked out the way I hoped, I could finish *Apocalypse Now* and go right to work on the set of *The Boys in Company C*.

That's pretty much what happened, but with an important new break for me: while I was waiting to get to work on *The Boys in Company C*, I got my first acting part. Coppola had returned from his fund-raising and started rolling on *Apocalypse Now* again. One day, I heard him say, "I need a helicopter pilot."

"You're looking at him!" I shouted, kicking my skills as a hustler into high gear.

Coppola decided to give me a shot. I went to the wardrobe department, got rigged up as a helicopter pilot, and sat down in the pilot's seat on the set. We did several takes, mostly with me ad-libbing as we went. Coppola would tell me the situation, like, "A VC vehicle is crossing the burning bridge, about to get away…Come up with something!" I would respond with my ad-lib lines.

My "takes" went into the movie. A star was born! It was a small part; any skilled actor would have been able to do it standing on his head. But…what the hell…so could I.

Apocalypse Now took about a year to complete, and when it was over, *The Boys in Company C* was in production. I literally went down the road a ways and onto the set to start my next big job as technical advisor.

Few, if any, writers in Hollywood have ever been in the military, much less the Marine Corps. Most of what they write, it seems to me, is stuff they've seen in military movies. So the technical advisor's job is to clean this crap up by studying the script, identifying what is fake or technically incorrect, and fixing it.

Naturally, conflicts arose on set, instances when the cameras were scheduled to roll but technical alarms had sounded. I would find something wrong with the script and seek out Sidney, saying, "Sid, this is kinda incorrect here. It really sucks. We have to fix this, because the action would never happen this way."

Sidney would throw up his hands. "Well, Jesus Christ. We're about to shoot. What the hell can we do about it?"

I was always prepared to answer that question. I would pull a sheaf of papers from my pocket, with the scene rewritten two or three ways, saying, "Here are a few options. Take your pick."

> **I didn't know it yet, but the next six words I was to hear would become the most important of my life. Nothing would be the same, ever again!**

I would even act the scene out for him. I would say things like, "Now I'm the squad leader. We're walking down this path. Ten paces apart here." I would go on, ad-libbing what I thought the dialogue should be.

Sidney liked what he saw and heard so much that the next thing I knew, I was playing the role of Sergeant Loyce. My preparations had paid off. I had shown Sidney I was capable of playing the part. Sid hadn't realized it, but I had been auditioning all along!

Now I had gotten myself a major role this time, in my second movie. I continued to ad-lib a lot when Sidney had the cameras rolling. It all worked, giving me a chance to excel. Hell, I had lived the role of Staff NCO in real life. I was a Drill Instructor in the Corps. Doing it in front of the camera came naturally for me. I played the role for the whole length of the movie.

Despite my technical advisor and acting credits, my beachhead in the movie business proved hard to expand. I came back to the States, made the rounds, but things had dried up in the movie business to the point where I had to seek a regular job.

That old paycheck thing again. Got to have one!

I got a job working at a nuclear power plant in Hanford, Washington. I had read the books and taken the tests and worked in quality assurance in HVAC (heating, ventilation, and air conditioning). I was married by then and living in a trailer house. I came home from work one day, and my wife said a movie director had called and said he would call back.

His name was Sid Furie. About an hour later, he was on the phone.

"Lee, I'm in the Philippines doing a movie called *Purple Hearts*, and I need you."

"Oh, boy!" I thought. "Here we go."

I gave the nuclear plant my two weeks' notice in my usual way, not wanting to burn any bridges, but they cut me free in one week, and I was on a plane heading for the Philippines once again. My wife threw a fit. I was making over twenty dollars per hour, good money back then in the eighties. We had two kids, and she wasn't happy with me leaving to chase my dream. But I had to go. I knew I didn't want to spend my life working at a nuclear power plant. Not when I knew I could still succeed as an actor. (My family never missed a meal, by the way. I did point that out to Mrs. Gunny.)

So off I went to the Philippines. Sidney Furie had sent me a ticket, and he met me at the airport. I worked on *Purple Hearts* with him for three months, both as technical advisor and in a small acting part. Then I was back home again, unemployed.

Even though I had been paid well and had money to hold out for a while as I sought new film work, I once again found my fledgling career in film on hold. I took work on another nuclear power plant, this time in Clinton, Illinois. I helped build that plant.

One day when I was home, the phone rang and I picked it up. I said, "Lee Ermey."

I didn't know it yet, but the next six words I was to hear would become the most important of my life. Nothing would be the same ever again!

The voice on the phone said, "Hello, Lee. This is Stanley Kubrick."

GUNNY'S RULES FOR
BEING PREPARED

✪ THE FIRST STEP TO SUCCESS: PLAN AHEAD

Being prepared is often simple, but it does take time and effort. You won't get anywhere by just pulling some random thoughts together at the last minute.

Say your mission is to go to a job interview or meeting. Can you discuss background facts, ask intelligent questions, and describe your own interests with enthusiasm and confidence? If you sit there with your mind a blank and your voice almost mumbling because you don't know what to say…well, you get the picture. Lack of preparation causes nervousness, making it obvious to everyone around you that you've screwed up. You'll be wishing you had been better prepared. And whatever your goal, you're probably going to lose out to someone who *was* prepared.

✪ AN ACTOR'S CODE: MEMORIZING LINES

Spencer Tracy once joked about acting, saying, "Just know your lines and don't bump into the furniture." In the world of filmmaking, almost nothing an actor does can top the shame and humiliation of being in front of the camera and not knowing the lines. Anywhere from a dozen to a hundred crew members, all pros, will be watching, doing their jobs, while the actor flubs the dialogue. From the director to every member of the crew, a lack of respect flares across the set. No matter how famous the actor is, his amateurish lack of preparation for his role is a confidence killer for the crew. Sometimes you have to shoot entire scenes over and over, all because Shit-Skull didn't know his lines.

From the first moment I ever stepped onto a movie set with lines to speak, I was determined to never let such embarrassment happen to me. And it never has! I know my lines. I prepare by copying them from the script several times. Then, when I can copy them from my memory and have them perfectly match the script, I know I've got them down cold.

⬛ THE BIG BREAK: ARE YOU READY?

When Furie asked my opinion on how we could salvage a scene in *The Boys in Company C*, my notes and my answers were ready. When a chance to play the helicopter pilot in *Apocalypse Now* suddenly appeared, I was ready to go for it. Both were big breaks, maybe even lucky breaks. But they were breaks I had been hoping—and preparing—for. My point is that when a break comes your way, you need to be prepared to latch onto it, squeeze it, work it for all its worth. If you're not prepared, you will probably be nervous—and you'll back away. You'll never know what might have been.

⬛ THE DEVIL DOG IS IN THE DETAILS: CHECKLISTS

When you're preparing for success, don't be afraid to use checklists to help you think ahead and be thorough. In many instances, these advance preparation tools are so important that they involve life-and-death details. Take checklists in aviation, shipping, and other high-tech ventures, for example. Or consider shifts of law enforcement officers going on duty, nurses and doctors switching shifts in the emergency room, or a patrol of soldiers or Marines going outside the wire in a battle zone. If their preparations are incomplete or screwed up, people may die. Most of us do not live in that kind of demanding operational mode, but the lesson is still relevant. When you're making decisions that may affect your life, be thorough and use checklists. Don't screw it up, Gomer!

⭐ TAKE PREPARATION SERIOUSLY OUT WHERE THE PAVEMENT ENDS

In 2012, a simple hike turned tragic when a father and his two sons died of exposure in a popular hiking trail area of a Missouri state forest. The father (an Air Force veteran, no less), his boys, and their Labrador retriever were out for a winter afternoon hike when darkness and a storm approached, and they became disoriented and took the wrong trail. Instead of heading toward their vehicle, they went deeper and deeper into the forest while night closed in, bringing bitterly cold rain.

The next day, the three were found dead of exposure, with the Lab still alive beside their bodies. Evidently, they were unable to make a fire or build shelter. They had no food and no warm clothing. They were reported to have been carrying a flashlight and cell phone—both with dead batteries.

This obvious lack of preparation cries out to us as a specific lesson: when you're headed into the wilderness, think ahead about what you might need in case you encounter an unexpected overnight situation—matches, knives, a flashlight, food bars, and a small first aid kit. Be prepared ahead of time with your own survival kit (it's actually fun to make up your own fanny pack, or hiking backpack, stocked with the stuff you need for the kind of country you're going into).

While we're on the topic of wilderness survival, there are a few questions I'd like to urge you to consider: Can you build a fire in the rain or in a wet forest? Can you make an overnight shelter using a knife, or machete, or hatchet? Can you use a compass and read a map? If you're heading for the backcountry, being prepared is also about knowing *how* to do these things. If you don't know, you can reach out to books, videos, and training courses to get squared away.

But this tragedy also calls our attention to the reality that no matter how short our mission is, we should always carry with us the essentials for staying alive. Whatever the situation—surviving in a forest, nailing a job interview, or whatever—it's far better to have what you need and then find you don't need it than it is to fail, or even perish, because you didn't take preparation seriously.

◼ THE BUG-OUT BAG, GUNNY STYLE

Hurricanes, earthquakes, tsunamis, floods. They all spell disaster and ruin, and any one of them can unleash pure hell and shut down civilized life where you live. When such bad luck comes roaring down The Gunny's street, he aims to put up a damned good fight, starting with a bug-out bag. I'm packing mine with everything I need to help my family and me to stay alive for as long as we can: lights, batteries, fire-starters, matches, portable stoves and fuel, firewood, MREs, bags of food staples, rain gear, firearms (for hunting *and* protection), extra ammo, knives and hatchets, and first aid kits. You can't pull all this stuff together *after* the quake or tsunami hits.

BE PREPARED
QUOTES WORTH REPEATING

"By failing to prepare, you are preparing to fail."

—Benjamin Franklin

"There is in the act of preparing, the moment you start caring."

—Winston Churchill

"Miracles come in moments. Be ready and willing."

—Wayne Dyer

"It's not the will to win that matters—everyone has that. It's the will to prepare to win that matters."

—Alabama football coach Paul "Bear" Bryant

"If I had eight hours to chop down a tree, I'd spend six sharpening my axe."

—Abraham Lincoln

"Luck is what happens when preparation meets opportunity."

—Seneca

"The future belongs to those who prepare for it."

—Ralph Waldo Emerson

"Before everything else, getting ready is the secret of success."

—Henry Ford

"You can map out a fight plan or a life plan, but when the action starts, it may not go the way you planned, and you're down to your reflexes—your training.

That's where your roadwork shows. If you cheated on that in the dark of morning, well, you're getting found out now, under the bright lights."

—Joe Frazier

"A goal without a plan is just a wish."

—Antoine de Saint-Exupéry

"Whatever failures I have known, whatever errors I have committed, whatever follies I have witnessed in private and public life have been the consequence of action without thought."

—Bernard M. Baruch

"He who every morning plans the transaction of the day and follows out that plan carries a thread that will guide him through the maze of the most busy life. But where no plan is laid, where the disposal of time is surrendered merely to the chance of incidence, chaos will soon reign."

—Victor Hugo

"Sometimes we have the dream but we are not ourselves ready for the dream. We have to grow to meet it."

—Louis L'Amour

"If you are prepared, you will be confident, and will do the job."

—Tom Landry

"If I miss a day of practice, I know it. If I miss two days, my manager knows it. If I miss three days, my audience knows it."

—André Previn

"I will prepare, and some day my chance will come."

—Abraham Lincoln

"What I do is prepare myself until I know I can do what I have to do."

—Joe Namath

"One of life's most painful moments comes when we must admit that we didn't do our homework, that we were not prepared."

—Merlin Olsen

CHAPTER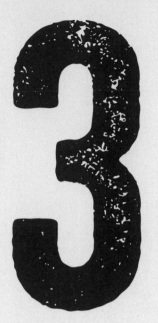

"HOLY JESUS! WHAT IS THAT? A JELLY DOUGHNUT?"

THE GUNNY MANIFESTO ON FITNESS AND HEALTH

Like I tried to tell Recruit Pyle in *Full Metal Jacket*, jelly doughnuts don't fit into our fitness program.

Vince D'Onofrio smiled at his reflection in the mirror, pleased with his seventy-pound weight gain. He wasn't just pudgy; he was becoming a blimp.

Great. That was just what his boss wanted. A disgusting fatbody! No, really.

Several months before, Vince was a handsome, young New York actor striving for success. Then his big break came. Legendary director Stanley Kubrick offered him a chance to play the pivotal role of Recruit Private Pyle in the movie *Full Metal Jacket*. The film was in production at Pinewood Studios outside London in 1986.

Vince would have to gain seventy pounds so he could play the role of a Marine recruit who was so overweight, physically inept, and screwed up in general that he stayed ever in the crosshairs of his Drill Instructor.

As Gunnery Sergeant Hartman, I tore into Private Pyle unmercifully. As R. Lee Ermey on the set, I considered Vince a friend, and I worked with him to share whatever acting tidbits I could pass on from my few years of experience.

Vince did a superb job as Private Pyle, and today I'm not at all surprised by his continuing success as an actor. He enjoyed a long run on the highly successful series *Law & Order*: *Criminal Intent*, which put him back in New York, where he started, and back down to a respectable weight once again.

If you get fat, you may not be able to get any work. And if you do get a job, you might not be able to do it.

Vince can have a jelly doughnut if he feels like it. However, when Gunnery Sergeant Hartman caught Private Pyle with a jelly doughnut, the Drill Instructor's tongue-lashing exploded through the barracks. Jelly doughnuts and Marines in fighting shape don't go together. In Marine talk, jelly doughnuts are fat pills.

Vince D'Onofrio got fat because he was an actor going to work. If *you* get that fat, you may not be able to get any work. And if you do get a job, you might not be able to do it. I damned sure wouldn't want you on my team.

Ever say this to yourself while standing in front of a mirror: "You look like hell!"?

I'm not talking about your wardrobe. I'm talking flab and fat. What the hell happened to you? What were you thinking while you let yourself go?

Fortunately, if you're reading this book, you haven't lost the war. Your poor physical condition hasn't killed you. Yet. You still have time to regroup and find a program that works for you.

Getting back in shape takes commitment and initiative—two ingredients missing in all those the magic-medicine-man, drug-peddler diets dangled in front of us every day, trying to lure us into the promise of losing weight without any effort, without having to give up a damn thing.

Commitment to fitness comes first, followed by initiating the right diet. And I'll bet you ten to one that the diet that ends up being the right one for you will not be one of the latest fads, the kind that make the best-seller lists every weekend. In waging my personal battle to stay in shape, and trying to whip hundreds of recruits into iron-bellied Marines, I've learned a thing or two, even though I'm not a professional fitness instructor, dietician, or corpsman. That said, if you want to get up the hills faster, I think I can help you.

The first two rules of Gunny's Fitness Manifesto are these:

Rule one: If you're overweight, guess what? You didn't gain all that weight overnight, and you are not going to lose it overnight either. I don't give a damn what the medicine-men phonies and fad-diet peddlers tell you. You need a realistic battle plan for the weeks or months it'll take to shed the flab and then a lifelong commitment to keep it off.

Rule two: Your diet can't be so severe that it defeats your commitment. If your diet makes you miserable, one day you're going to say, "The hell with it!"

But giving up is for losers, not for those of us who want to be squared away, capable, and prepared—lean, mean fighting machines.

So set your goals. You don't have to look like a professional athlete, or a movie star, or a model, or a combat-ready Marine. But you sure as heck want to feel healthy and energized—and look the part, too. Looking heavy and out of shape is not the image you want to project. Feeling heavy and out of shape is not the life you want to lead. And with all the information and resources available—the internet, books, magazines, groups like Weight Watchers, television shows, DVDs, and entire channels dedicated to weight loss and health and wellness—there really is no excuse for anyone to be a fat-body these days unless there are medical conditions a person can't overcome.

Hell, I don't know which program's right for you, but I can tell you what's worked for me and what works in the Marines. In the Marine Corps recruit fitness programs of my Drill Instructor days, the fat kids were given no diet choices. We basically put them on the salad bar, and they grazed on rabbit food. We worked them so physically hard all day, every day, that the pounds came off like ice cream melting in the sun.

At the opposite pole from the hardcore Marine recruit diet is one that I admire for its simplicity—and results. This one is based on calorie counting, once the supreme law of weight control but now a method the diet gurus kick around like a soccer ball. In the "calories count!" world, consuming more calories than you burn means you'll gain weight. Burning more than you consume means you'll lose weight. It's common sense, and what it generally means is that if you cut five hundred calories from your diet (or burn them off through exercise), you'll lose a pound a week. It might seem slow at first, but it works. It's simple math, after all.

Sensible fitness programs and balancing diet with exercise work a lot better than fads like the "Hollywood Grapefruit Diet" and those that have you totally eliminate key elements of nutrition, like carbohydrates and fat. Your body needs some carbs and some fat, in moderation. And it needs exercise. Be aware, however, that exercise alone cannot wipe out a bad diet.

As a Marine and professional actor, I've been in a state of high alert all my life when it comes to fitness and my appearance. To be a Marine with a weight problem was unthinkable; it would have shamed me to death in my beloved Corps.

Feeling fit and energized is a reward worth whatever it takes to attain.

To be a pudgy actor showing up to audition for the kinds of roles I like to play would have been a ticket to the unemployment line.

I've *had* to stay fit—or go out of business!

Not that I'm bitching about having to watch calories and work out; in fact, I'm here to tell you that feeling fit and energized is a reward worth whatever it takes to attain. Though I'm not the lean and mean Devil Dog I was back when I was on active duty in the Marine Corps, I can still get up the hill. Because I watch my diet and make exercise a religion, the few pounds my slowing metabolism has let slip through the wire are not a problem. I'm healthy!

When I'm hunting in places like Africa or closer to home in the high-country West, I can still hump it right alongside the guides, whether I'm tracking on foot or even jogging in pursuit of big game.

I love to play golf, and I'm posting scores in the high eighties or low nineties. I'm still driving the ball 250 yards off the tee, even if I do have to contend with a few aches and pains from a hip that feels like it's going bad, and my old shoulder injury that won't let me throw a ball overhead or play tennis as much as I'd like to. But my sidearm works fine. I'm good to go.

Not long ago, at an event at a Smoky Mountain Knife Works show in Tennessee, I stood greeting folks for twelve straight hours without sitting down, making a head call, eating, or taking a break. I'm used to long sessions like that for GLOCK, SOG, Tru-Spec, and Victory Motorcycles.

When I'm on the road, I work out doing isometrics in my room. I find that when I visit exercise facilities in hotels, I end up spending most of my time talking with folks who recognize me and want to chat—something I also love to do, but I have to guard my workout time no matter what. And isometrics are simple, easy, and effective— it's sort of like weight lifting without weights, simply contracting for a set period of time (ten seconds per repetition, for instance) the muscle you want to work as if moving a weight. Marine Lieutenant Colonel W. H. Rankin wrote a book on isometrics called *Be Fit as a Marine* that you can still pick up in used bookstores and that can get you started, but really all you need is some imagination. An easy example: flex your right bicep, put the base of your left fist in the palm of your right hand, and push the fist down while the palm tries to come up, flexing the bicep harder. Hold for ten seconds and repeat. Another good move is known in the Marines as The Electric Chair. Put your back against the wall, squat down until your legs are at 90 degrees and then hold it for as long as you can. Extend your arms at your side, palms against the wall, and push for a little extra back and arm action while you're squatting. One important thing is to never hold your breath. If you don't keep breathing, it puts too much strain on your body, and bad things can happen. After you've done an isometric routine hitting all the major muscles in the body, it's a good idea to stretch out. Especially as we get older, keeping flexibility gets tougher. You have to work at it.

As for chow, I find that, within reason, I can eat pretty much what I want—as long as I put in time on my treadmill.

My favorite exercise session is one hour on the treadmill. What works best for me is getting on that damned old treadmill and putting one foot in front of the other while watching *The O'Reilly Factor*. When I'm home, I use dumbbells and barbells for strength training.

I also still like jogging in my combat boots despite some of the warnings you hear from some medical people that jogging is bad for your legs. Bullshit! Look at basketball players. Look at me. I've been doing it all my life. You decide.

Watch the clock. Set a goal for yourself: a certain time, a certain speed. Start with, say, fifteen minutes at a certain grade. After four or five days, move up to twenty minutes. You have to keep moving your goals—you want to improve, not get stuck in a rut.

Eventually, you should be able to jog—whether on the track, road, or treadmill—for one hour. That's the goal. One hour. When you can do that, you'll be fit. Cardio strong. And it's good for your coconut, too, a real booster shot to brainpower (and pride)!

Walking is a great exercise alternative. In fact, it's so effective in maintaining fitness and can be such a pleasant experience that many people make walking their exercise of choice. They can afford a treadmill if they want one, and they have access to gyms, but they're out there walking instead. Golfers who walk the course know all about the pleasures and benefits of walking. They're getting in about a six-mile walk in eighteen holes of golf. And, unless you're upset by your scorecard, golf courses are beautiful places to take a walk.

For young people, my fitness message goes double.

Being out of shape when you're young can really mess up your life. You won't look capable, like an achiever. Being fat makes you look lazy and listless. First impressions will be against you. I'm a firm believer that to be successful in this life, you need to be physically fit and look smart. Take pride in your appearance!

And you know why? Because employers look at someone who looks fit and squared away and think, "Now there's someone with self-discipline, self-respect, a work ethic, who's got it together. That's the sort of person we want on our team." Employers look for people who are dependable, enthusiastic, and creative. They want people with energy and drive. Who wants to hire a sickly, lazy-ass slob?

> **You've got to get that body into the kind of shape where you can stand naked in front of a full-length mirror and say to yourself, "You're looking good, dude!"**

Some people spend thousands of dollars on a wardrobe and hang it on a weak, fat, sorry-looking body. You've got to get that body into the kind of shape where you can stand naked in front of a full-length mirror and say to yourself, "You're looking good, dude!" Then you'll have pride and confidence—and energy, ambition, and success will follow.

When you put on some decent clothes and head out for job interviews or sales, people will think, "This guy looks after himself. This guy is motivated. This guy is squared away." And who doesn't want that?

I mentioned "messing up your life." Booze and drugs are the fast tracks for doing exactly that. Alcohol and drugs destroy more careers and marriages than you can imagine in your wildest dreams. I've seen it happen again and again.

I drank some when I was a young Marine. I gave it up years ago. Being a smart man, I could see what it was doing to me. I don't mean it's a bad choice; it's a stupid choice. Because the writing's on the wall:

with too much booze in your body, bad things are going to happen to you.

I'm not what they call a teetotaler. I'll have a beer with the NCOs every now and then. I even invested in starting a microbrewery recently, and every now and then I try the product in moderation.

But that's the extent of my drinking. I get along nicely without it.

If you're the type who likes to finish the day with a beer or two, or even a drink or two or a glass of wine or two, and then call it quits, no big deal. But if one or two isn't enough, and you keep drinking, you're in trouble, whether you admit it or not. You need help, and you'd better pull yourself together before booze tears your life to shreds.

If you don't believe me, go down to your county courthouse, as I do sometimes, and take a good look around. You'll see the wreckage of alcohol and drugs strewn about before your very eyes.

Whenever I'm at a party or gathering and I hear people starting to slur their words, I start thinking about bailing. For sure, when the "I love you, man!" bullshit starts, I'm out the door.

I've had enough boozers in my life, starting with my father, a recovered alcoholic.

I hope I've said enough about the subject for you to take heed. And I sincerely hope you'll put what I've said into your coconut and keep it there.

Out in "Hollyweird," as I call it, when I've got a film in production, I'm surrounded by some of the best-looking men and women on the planet. Often, even the ones who are well known for their drinking or drugging manage to pull themselves together to look great when it's "showtime."

I don't have to worry about "showtime" coming down. I'm always ready. I step into my roles feeling confident, prepared, and physically top-notch. My commitment to fitness through diet and exercise rewards me with vitality and backs up my professionalism. When I go to trade shows and meet hundreds of people who have been standing in line, I laugh and joke with every one, taking time with them. I can only do that because I feel great.

If you've been putting in too much couch time, letting fitness and vitality slip away, let me tell you, you'll feel a helluva lot better and kick butt in your work and play if you start working out and eating right.

GUNNY'S RULES ON
FITNESS AND HEALTH

★ DON'T KID YOURSELF. CALORIES COUNT!

You don't have to be an Einstein to figure out that if you eat three full meals a day with perhaps a snack in between and don't exercise…well, dude, you're going to be a fat pig. And it's going to get worse every year as your metabolism slows with aging.

★ GOT MILK? I SURE AS HELL HAVE!

If I have an addiction, it's milk. I drink a half gallon to a full gallon every day. It has to be fat-free organic. I love the taste, and it refreshes me. On the road, I stop at a grocery store on the way to the hotel to make sure I have my milk, since I like to end my day with a cold glass or two. Don't try to tell me that milk isn't good for you. Fatty types, maybe, if you're worried about cholesterol. Not my fat-free organic. I grew up on a farm, drinking milk, I'm drinking it now, and I'm going to continue paying no attention whatsoever to those people who say milk isn't good for you.

✪ A COMMENT ON SMOKING

If you're still smoking, you've lost your freaking mind! Enough said.

✪ NO PAIN, NO GAIN?

I believe in that old adage. When I was a lot younger than I am now, I could run marathons on the beach. When I hit that "wall," where going on seemed impossible, I could lock the pain out of my mind. Of course, that was some very serious conditioning going on.

I'm not trying to pretend I'm still in my thirties, but I still like to push myself a bit in my workouts and challenge my body. I also believe in varying the workout with "hard day, easy day" drills.

✪ CADENCE CALLS: SHOUT 'EM OUT!

As most military recruits have learned, nothing puts a spring in your step when jogging quite like the sound of a cadence being called by a Drill Instructor. Some of the most popular cadences of the Vietnam War years are shouted out by Gunnery Sergeant Hartman in *Full Metal Jacket*. Though most of them are R-rated, one you might remember is not:

> I don't want no teenage queen,
> I just want my M-16.

During World War II, a popular cadence emerged in dozens of variations referring to a mysterious guy named Jody. He's the guy who stayed behind and is now dating your girl, living the good life while you went to war for your country. As I said in my *Mail Call* television series and book, I barked a helluva lot of Jodies in my day, but here is one of my favorites:

> Ain't no use in going back,
> Jody's got your Cadillac.
> Ain't no use in calling home,
> Jody's got your girl and gone.
> Ain't no use in feeling blue,
> Jody's got your sister too!

You can find all the cadences you'll ever want to hear on the internet today, including those recorded for your running pleasure with iPods and headphones.

★ GUNNY'S SWEET SIXTEEN

The Marines used to have a "daily seven" exercises that were eventually replaced by the "daily sixteen," which can be used as a warm-up to a workout or done as a workout in itself. There are plenty of places to find the daily sixteen and how to use them, including the aptly named book, *The Marine Corps Daily 16 Workouts: Marine Fitness for the Civilian Athlete*, but here's a sweet, simple, and effective workout that anyone can do, anywhere, with no equipment—you can call it the "Gunny Sweet Sixteen." I'm no licensed doctor or physical therapist, but this will do the job if you work at your own pace.

1. First, warm up with some side-straddle hops (that's jumping jacks to you)—thirty usually does the trick.

2. Then, do some alternating leg lunges, stepping forward with your front leg at a right angle, your rear leg also at a right angle, with your rear knee nearly touching the floor. Do at least ten each side.

3. Do some arm swings front and back. Ten front, ten back will work.

4. Push-ups (max reps).

5. Sit-ups or crunches or any variation thereof (max reps).

6. Supermen (lying on belly, lifting your arms and legs for a three count; at least 10 reps).

7. Push-ups (max reps).

8. Sit-ups or sit-up variation, with opposite elbow hitting opposite knee (max reps).

9. Supermen (at least 10 reps).

10. Push-ups (max reps).

11. Sit-ups or variation (max reps).

12. Supermen (at least ten).

13. Pull-ups (if you have a pull-up bar handy) or triceps push-ups (hands under your chest with thumbs and forefingers touching forming a triangle; max reps).

14. Leg lifts (feet off the ground six inches, raise them to forty-five degrees then back down to six inches; max reps).

15. Eight-count body builders (from standing position, jump down and kick out to a push-up position, do a push-up, kick your feet out wide, kick 'em back up in, kick up to a squat, then jump in the air…and do it all over again for at least ten reps).

16. Go for a thirty- to sixty-minute run.

All this workout requires is that you give it your best, whether that's ten push-ups a set or fifty or whatever. Anybody can do it, and anyone can benefit from it. Ooorah!

✪ NO SODA, THANK YOU

I don't drink soda—no Coke, no Pepsi, and not even the low-calorie or no-calorie kinds. I prefer the low-cal fruit-flavored waters. Some of them are tasty. If there are none around and I'm thirsty, I'll take plain water. Of course, a cold glass of my fat-free organic milk is always welcome.

✪ THE LOST PLEASURE OF BATHS

Unless I'm in a hurry to meet a schedule, my days at home begin with a one- or two-hour bath. The water is as hot as I can stand it, and I have a special tub I've had built to allow me to prop myself back at a comfortable position and read my current favorite book. I'm no Winston Churchill, who began his days in a similar manner, but I've found the bath does wonders for smoothing out the kinks that have built up during my days on the road. Sometimes when I go back to my hotel after a day of greeting people at trade shows, I find a hot bath to be the perfect relaxing way to end my day.

✪ MAKING TIME

There's an old cliché that says, "People who say they don't have time to exercise actually don't have time *not* to." As in many clichés, there's a lot of truth in that one. Let's face it: You find time to do everything else that needs to be done in your life; surely you can make room for some exercise in one form or another. Stop putting off your workout with the excuse that you don't have time. Give exercise a high priority in your life, and you'll find a way to make time.

★ MY BREAKFAST BOOSTER

Every morning when I'm home, Mrs. Gunny prepares a special health-drink concoction for me. She uses the blender to mix an eight-ounce drink of celery, wheatgrass, garlic, radish, flaxseed, raspberries, and enough water to make it drinkable. It's not FDA approved, but it works for me.

★ AVOIDING AIRPORT STRESS

I travel so much that avoiding stress at the airports I visit is an absolute priority. I try to do that by arriving for my flight far ahead of the required time. Then I sit and relax with my book or browse the bookstores and magazine racks for a while. I completely eliminate that uptight feeling of people I see scurrying to make it to the gates on time.

HEALTH AND FITNESS
QUOTES WORTH REPEATING

"We do not stop exercising because we grow old. We grow old because we stop exercising."
—Dr. Kenneth Cooper, Cooper Institute

"An early-morning walk is a blessing for the whole day."
—Henry David Thoreau

"Those who think they have no time for bodily exercise will sooner or later have to find time for illness."

—Edward Stanley

"The reason that I can be 38 and have two kids and wear a bikini is because I work my [expletive] ass off. It's not luck, it's not fairy dust, it's not good genes. It's killing myself for an hour and a half five days a week."

—Gwyneth Paltrow

"Walking is the best possible exercise. Habituate yourself to walk very far."

—Thomas Jefferson

"An active mind cannot exist in an inactive body."

—General George S. Patton Jr.

"Physical fitness can neither be achieved by wishful thinking nor outright purchase."

—Joseph Pilates

"If your dog is too fat, you're not getting enough exercise."

—Anonymous

"Self-delusion is pulling in your stomach when you step on the scales."

—Paul Sweeney

"Take care of your body. It's the only place you have to live."

—Jim Rohn

"Aerobics: a series of strenuous exercises which help convert fats, sugars, and starches into aches, pains, and cramps."

—Anonymous

"Suck it up!"

—Anonymous

"Worrying about gray hair when your weight's soaring out of control is like mowing your lawn while your house is on fire."

—Edward Ugel

"When it comes to eating right and exercising, there is no 'I'll start tomorrow.' Tomorrow is disease."

—Terri Guillemets

"Movement is a medicine for creating change in a person's physical, emotional, and mental states."

—Carol Welch

"No matter who you are, no matter what you do, you absolutely, positively do have the power to change."

—Bill Phillips

"A vigorous five-mile walk will do more good for an unhappy but otherwise healthy adult than all the medicine and psychology in the world."

—Dr. Paul Dudley White

"Physical fitness is not only one of the most important keys to a healthy body, it is the basis of dynamic and creative intellectual activity."

—President John F. Kennedy

"What fits your busy schedule better, exercising one hour a day or being dead twenty-four hours a day?"

—Randy Glasbergen, cartoonist

CHAPTER **4**

"GO THE EXTRA MILE"

HUMPING IT BEYOND WHAT IS EXPECTED OF YOU

When failure is not an option, there's no quitting time!

Stanley Kubrick said, "No."

The famed director told me he would not give me an audition for the role of Drill Instructor Hartman in *Full Metal Jacket*. He already had his Hartman cast, test-filmed, contracted, and set to go. He had hired me to come to England to serve as technical advisor on the film, and that was it.

We were in his office on the set of *Full Metal Jacket* at Pinewood Studios outside London. I had joined the film company only a short time before, but I fully expected my bid to audition to be met with success. I had positioned myself for acting roles in my three previous movies—*Apocalypse Now*, *The Boys in Company C*, and *Purple Hearts*—and I thought I could do it again. This time, the stakes were even higher. The role of Gunnery Sergeant Hartman was to die for.

Back when he had called me at my home in Illinois, Stanley had never mentioned any possibility that I might play Gunnery Sergeant Hartman. The idea was entirely a product of my own ambition.

Our telephone conversation had started with Stanley saying, "Hello, Lee. This is Stanley Kubrick."

I had thought, "Yeah, right." It was some guy from the office dicking around with me, I suspected. Stanley Kubrick was one of the hottest directors in the world, with films like *2001: A Space Odyssey*, *Spartacus*, and *The Shining*.

"No, no, it's really Stanley Kubrick," he said. "I'm making a new movie. Have you ever heard of a book called *The Short-Timers*, by Gustav Hasford?"

"Heard of it?" I replied. "I'm reading it right now for the second time." I told him I thought it was a great book but was filled with inaccurate bullshit.

Right away, I had his attention. "What do you mean?" he said, openly startled. "Can you give me an example of that?"

"I can do better than that," I said. "I'll write you an outline of the book and send it to you."

Stanley told me he had been watching a lot of Vietnam movies, and my name kept cropping up. He had talked to Sid Furie about me and gotten my number from him.

The "outline" I promised Stanley became a twenty-page book report that I Express Mailed to him ASAP. About a week and a half later, I got the call.

"Lee, we would like you to join the film as technical advisor. How much do you want?"

More important to me than the money was the opportunity. Once in England to work on the movie, I did not allow Stanley's rejection of my auditioning for the Drill Instructor role to last very long.

The Marine Corps had not taught me to establish a beachhead, then give it up.

The Marine Corps had not taught me to roll over and play dead.

I immediately came up with Plan Baker.

I had been working closely on the film with Stanley's number one assistant, Leon Vitali, who had been in Stanley's movie *Barry Lyndon*. Leon and Stanley were really tight. To me, he seemed more like a son to Stanley than an assistant. Leon and I were getting along so well that I thought I could ask him for a favor.

We were about to start selecting and videotaping candidates to be background extras in the film. Stanley had to approve every last detail of the picture, including still-shots of the prospective extras and our videotapes. I explained to the recruits when I lined them up in platoon formation that I was going to come at them like a true Drill Instructor. "It won't be personal," I warned them. "Forget what I will be saying about your mothers and fathers."

"It won't be personal. Forget what I will be saying about your mothers and fathers."

I showed up wearing the DI Smokey Bear cover I had picked up from our wardrobe department, and since I wore the Marine Corps trousers and duty belt every day, I looked the part. With Leon on the video camera, taping the candidates for Stanley's benefit, I started working down the row. I had people with their pants down at their knees, people sucking their thumbs, people doing pushups. After a couple of minutes, I noticed Leon had stopped focusing on the recruits and was pointing the camera at me. I thought, "Yes. This is working."

I only stopped when the camera ran out of tape.

I knew that Leon would give the tape to Stanley, and that he would be looking at it late that night. He did that every night, reviewing the day's work.

The next morning, sure enough, I had a call right away to report to the production office. When I walked in, Stanley was sitting there with the kind of big old shit-eating grin on his face that only he could muster.

"You fucking sly old fox," he said. "I want you to play Gunnery Sergeant Hartman. How much do you want?"

I told him I only wanted him to be fair. "That's all I ask." I left it in his hands.

Stanley paid off the contract of the actor he had slated to play Hartman. What was a great break for R. Lee Ermey was a bad break for the other fellow, who was actually given another role in the movie. He played the helicopter door gunner, shouting, "Get some!" over and over as he machine-gunned the landscape. (I would not, by the way, be revealing this sensitive aspect of the Hartman casting had it not already been published in Matthew Modine's book, "*Full Metal Jacket*" *Diary*, and in the John Baxter biography of Stanley Kubrick. But as it's already out there as public knowledge, I can confirm it. It was obviously the biggest break of my movie career.)

I had gone the extra mile and found great reward. Stanley Kubrick went on to make the movie with me in the role of Gunnery Sergeant Hartman. The role was mine, but I knew that in working with a dedicated filmmaker like Stanley Kubrick, many more extra miles lay ahead.

I also continued as technical advisor for the film, and it was those duties that occupied me in the first months of production. The boot camp scenes where I do my thing as DI Hartman in the first part of the movie were actually shot last. The actors needed hair in the Vietnam scenes, and Stanley Kubrick was not one to use wigs. The first months of work on *Full Metal Jacket* were devoted to the Vietnam action. Set planning, set building and decoration, and the actual shooting took months. The sets were scattered over the English landscape and at the dilapidated, abandoned Beckton Gas Works buildings where the climactic battle scenes were filmed, complete with fires and explosions.

My acting scenes could wait. Every day, I was on duty working on countless details to help Stanley bring the Vietnam War to the screen. When the camera was following Papillon Soo, the Da Nang hooker, as she sashays in a mini-skirt and high pumps toward Joker's table, I could sense Stanley's genius happening in full force. Eventually, with Nancy Sinatra's "These Boots Are Made for Walkin'" as background music, the scene formed an unforgettable opening to part two of the movie. Throughout the weeks and months of Vietnam filming, I had complete confidence that Stanley was creating an unequaled work of art about Vietnam.

In fulfilling my mission as technical advisor in *Full Metal Jacket*, I was duty bound to make every scene in the picture 100 percent accurate. Guns and gear, troop movements, combat tactics—even the dialogue: it all had to be Marine-real, Vietnam-real. My personal knowledge and experiences were backed up by a long list of phone numbers of Sergeants major and Lieutenant Colonels with boots-on-ground duty in the kinds of combat zones we were recreating. I kept the phone lines from England to far-flung Marine Corps posts around the world busy with queries and checklists to nail down every detail I needed to give Stanley the "good-to-go" on every scene. Combat operations vary among Marine Corps units, so when I had conflicting opinions, I went with the majority. My Marine Corps contacts became "assistant technical advisors," so I wasn't limited to my own personal experience, but could give Stanley a well-rounded view, and give it with absolute confidence.

At one point, Stanley said to me, "Lee, you're the hardest working person on this picture." Then he thought for a moment, and added, "Except for me!"

> **It's not that Stanley wasn't a team player. He was. But it had to be *his* team. He had to call the shots.**

He was right about that: Stanley Kubrick kicked butt from before daylight until long after dark. When working on a film, he was a driven man, obsessed with details, making every scene come alive in his own particular vision.

Pinewood Studios and the scattered sets were his workplace, but Stanley also had a home life of considerable warmth and opulence. The family lived on a huge estate that included everything from gardens and grounds to stables and a house hundreds of years old. He had made England his home and Pinewood his base of operations for years, and he seemed totally at ease there, on his great keep, his fortress. He was sometimes ostracized by Hollywood and its moguls, particularly at Academy Awards time, for not playing ball, for living a separatist life. But he would not kiss the asses of any studio bosses who tried to tell him how to shoot his movies or what they should cost.

"Lee," Stanley told me one day. "Those old farts at the Academy wouldn't know a good movie, an artistic film, if it came up and took a shit in their mouths."

It's not that Stanley wasn't a team player. He was. But it had to be *his* team. He had to call the shots.

Everybody working for Stanley Kubrick knew that if they didn't go the extra mile, they would soon be on a plane, going home.

Stanley's creative integrity had survived films with powerful actors like Kirk Douglas (who was also a producer on *Spartacus*), Jack Nicholson, Sir Laurence Olivier, and many others. He also maintained an even keel when under fire by studio bosses, producers, and bean-counters who wanted things done their way—which mostly meant faster and cheaper. The man's filmmaking record shows him to have been virtually fearless, taking on all challengers, making his movies *his* way.

At one point during the filming of *Full Metal Jacket*, he actually had a producer sent by Warner Brothers barred from the set. The man had been sent to more or less snoop around and see how things were going.

Nobody pushed Stanley Kubrick around. Nobody!

Stanley attacked the making of *Full Metal Jacket* like a General setting out on a great campaign. First, he had built, sparing no detail, a table of miniatures of the exact sets we would build to shoot the movie. On these, he could plot every angle and visualize how the final sets were to be built and decorated.

Sets, cameras, lighting, acting—in every aspect of making the movie, Stanley had a crew of top-drawer professionals. Cinematographer Doug Milsome and his camera crew were as solid as they came. The same was true with sets and lighting. Yet, sometimes Stanley manned the camera himself, and always he was on top of every set and lighting decision. He literally could do every job the people he hired were doing.

An example of his focus occurred one morning when he was at the wheel of his wife's brand-new Mercedes, surveying possible camera locations at the Epping Forest. Stanley had me sit in the front seat, and Doug Milsome, Terry Needham (the first assistant director), and

Leon Vitali were in the back. We were moving very slowly down the road, alongside a ditch that was six feet deep.

Stanley's driving abilities were marginal, since it was something he seldom did, and on this occasion he was paying no attention to driving but was focused on where we might put the cameras.

"Terry," he said, pointing across the ditch toward the forest, "I want four cameras. Put the number one camera over there by that tree…another over there. I want slow-mo as well. How soon can you get base camp set up here and have the troops charging across that field in full combat gear?"

Terry said that he would have to get the company's lunch out of the way first, then move the wardrobe truck. He could have them ready by three o'clock.

Stanley went on pointing and talking about the camera positions with such intensity that he let the Mercedes drift into the ditch and roll over, onto its side. Nobody seemed hurt. Stanley turned the ignition off and said, "What the hell are we sitting here for? Let's go."

I got my window open and climbed out. Standing on the side of the vehicle, I got the doors open and then helped everybody clamber out. Stanley was still talking about the shots, still gesturing. "Come on," he said, jumping onto the road and starting for our base camp, about a mile away. "We'll finish chow and get right back here. I want them charging across there by three o'clock."

We trudged along for a few more minutes, with Stanley still talking about the shots, when he finally, almost as an afterthought, turned and said, "And, Terry, have somebody come out here and see about that car."

As usual, Stanley was thinking about only one thing: his movie.

When I was lucky enough to get the job working with Stanley Kubrick on *Full Metal Jacket*, I knew his filmmaking wisdom and talent were renowned worldwide. My job was to help him make the military accuracy of the film second to none, and I tackled that with a 24/7 attitude and balls-to-the-wall effort. After four months, the Vietnam portions of the film were in the can, with the exception of the scene depicting the death of the sniper. That would be shot later on a special set at Pinewood Studios.

In January 1986, it was finally time for me to step in front of the cameras as Gunnery Sergeant Hartman. The boot camp sets were ready. The actors' heads were shaved and their uniforms were changed from Vietnam combat gear to boot camp trousers and buttoned collars.

Joker, Pyle, Cowboy, Eightball—all the recruits—were now going to receive the reaming out of their lives.

In the first weeks of the boot camp filming, I screamed so loudly and often that I lost my voice a couple of times. When that happened, Stanley had to shoot around me and wait patiently until my Hartman commands were back to full strength. Then I resumed playing the ultimate shock-and-awe Drill Instructor, so in-the-face real that when I slap Vince D'Onofrio (Pyle) on camera, the action jolts the audience, even though Vince was never smacked. I did actually slap Matthew Modine (Joker) a couple of times at his request. He wanted more realism in the shot to ramp up his reaction. The cameras were rolling; the movie was working.

In March, I was perched atop the "Stairway to Heaven" ladder on the set of the boot camp obstacle course at Bassingbourn airfield. I was chewing out Pyle as he tried to get over the top. He not only could not make it over, but Vince D'Onofrio suddenly developed a fear of heights and found himself frozen, twenty-some feet off the ground. He was unable to go either up or down. I had plenty enough acting experience from my other films to know that with three cameras running in elaborate cherry-picker setups, I had to come up with ad-lib dialogue and some kind of action to make the scene work. We managed to do that, with me chewing out Vince as we walked him back to the ground, and it saved the scene.

Stanley had us shooting near the end of the day for dramatic lighting, so that was the end of the day's filming. I hung around after dark, discussing the next day's schedule with Stanley, making sure everything would be ready.

It started to snow as I drove toward home in the bitter cold of the March evening. I stopped and picked up a large pizza for the family, then hurried on my way, headlights stabbing into the whirling flakes. My route carried me through the Epping Forest, where disaster struck. I hit a patch of invisible "black ice," and the little VW Rabbit spun out of control, careening onto a golf course and slamming into a tree.

Unable to move, pinned in the wreckage, I was dazed, but conscious, aware of the smashed windshield and the snow blowing into what was left of the car. As luck would have it, I had taken off my field jacket. I knew I was hurt bad. The darkness closed in from all sides. I was alone in a busted car with a busted body, off the road, out of sight of passing vehicles. I had to have help, or I was going to die right there, alone in the cold and dark, injured and freezing.

Gradually, when I could move my legs, I saw the flare of the taillights coming on when my foot touched the brake pedal. I began pressing on the pedal, back and to, back and to. The taillights were coming on and off, the glow blinking through the falling snow. The cold burned into my aching body. Would hypothermia kill me? How long could I hold on?

Eventually, after I had been there over two hours, a passerby saw the lights out on the golf course where they did not belong and stopped to check it out. There were no cell phones, so by the time my Good Samaritan got ahold of the rescue people, considerably more time had gone by. The paramedics pried me from the car and got me to the hospital. There, the doctors worked on my injuries and got me to a stabilized condition.

Gunnery Sergeant Hartman was in deep-shit trouble.

My life was out of danger, but the inventory of my smashed-up body told me, through a blur of pain, that my acting career was in serious danger, perhaps even finished. I had six broken ribs, a concussion, a dislocated shoulder, a dislocated hip, and a broken collarbone.

Gunnery Sergeant Hartman was in deep-shit trouble.

The next morning when Stanley walked into my room, his face carried the wry little grin that was a trademark expression when he was squared away.

"Lee," Stanley said, coming close to my bed, "Don't worry about the movie. I'm closing the production down for whatever time it takes for you to get back on your feet. Two months…three. This is why we have insurance."

I breathed a sigh of relief that must have been audible. Closing down a movie production was a huge deal, as I had already seen in the Philippines when the typhoon shut down *Apocalypse Now*.

Once again I had been redeemed. Once again, I had been given a fresh chance.

"When you feel like it, we'll work on the script together," Stanley went on. "We'll use the time we have."

And we did.

As you will see in the next chapter, "Major Malfunctions," we turned our setback into a triumph of will and work.

From the moment I had offered to write an outline of *The Short-Timers* for Stanley, I had gone the extra mile for him. He always did the same for me.

That was the way we lived. It was a partnership.

GUNNY'S RULES FOR
GOING THE EXTRA MILE

★ MAKE IT A HABIT

I said earlier that the Marines did not teach me to roll over and play dead in the tough spots. I have not always achieved my mission, but when I have come up short, it isn't because I do not go the extra mile, do not carry my load. I'll hump it as far as it takes to get what I want. I have done that every day of my life since I became a Marine, in large roles or meager ones, and I expect to continue doing it until I'm in a wheelchair or my trip is over.

★ THE QUITTERS AND LOSERS

Unfortunately, for many people the "extra mile" seems to be a distance they cannot make. You can spot them a mile away: the clock-watchers, the early quitters, the "wait till tomorrow" addicts, the "it's good enough, let's move on" cop-out artists. They're in every office, every organization, even units of the military, law enforcement, and elsewhere. They're not going to lift their hands one inch beyond their job descriptions, and often not even that far. I have no respect for these misguided hangers-on.

★ FAMILY MATTERS NEED ATTENTION

Families require "extra mile" performance as much as, if not more than, the workplace. Family cohesiveness and function depend on squared away, unwavering involvement between every member. The care, the love that cranks up families and keeps them going isn't just mama's job. There's usually something happening all the time that takes extra effort. We all care about our parents and our brothers and sisters. When it takes an extra mile to help the family get up the hill, we need to make damn sure we're not on leave or AWOL.

★ TAKING CARE OF "NUMBER ONE"

All those chores and things you've been putting off doing for yourself aren't going to stop bugging you until you call a halt and turn-to. You need to give your personal needs an extra mile at times to stay squared away. Your job and duties and the needs of others still rank high in your priorities, but you also have to look out for Number One. Sometimes that takes extra effort, whether it's getting in that hour-long run you need or taking care of a personal chore like shining your shoes or ironing your shirt. You're responsible to your family and your employer, but also to yourself.

★ THE BEST "EXTRA MILE" STORY I KNOW

A strikingly handsome (we're talking movie-star handsome) young man of Italian descent, John Basilone grew up in the quiet little town of Raritan, New Jersey, alongside the vast 2,000-acre estate of tobacco heiress Doris Duke. Before joining the Marines in 1940, he had already served a hitch in the Army with duty in the Philippines. When he went into action at Guadalcanal in the early days of World War II in 1942, Basilone carried the nickname "Manila John" among his fellow Leathernecks.

In a banzai attack that began at nighttime on his machinegun section's cut-off position at the airstrip called Henderson Field on Guadalcanal, Manila John and his unit held against a Japanese regiment for three days and nights—without rest or food. Basilone used two machineguns and his .45, sometimes cradling one machinegun in his arms. Only three Marines from Basilone's unit were still standing when the fight ended. During the action, Marines had to clear stacked Japanese bodies for fields of fire. Their hands were severely burned by their sizzling hot weapons.

As the first Marine to be awarded the Medal of Honor in World War II, Basilone toured the United States, promoting and selling war bonds. He fell in love with a beautiful lady, also a Marine, and they married. He could have continued in safe duties training troops and enjoying married life for the rest of the war. Manila John said "No!" to that.

About ninety minutes after the first waves of Marines hit the black lava beaches of Iwo Jima, Gunnery Sergeant John Basilone and his machinegun platoon were pinned down by torrents of enemy fire. Basilone rallied his men to get off the beach. They flanked a heavily fortified blockhouse and attacked it with grenades and demolitions, wiping out that Japanese strongpoint and its defending garrison. The Marines moved on toward the airfield through intense fire and minefields, assaulting enemy positions. Later in the day, Japanese gunfire cut Basilone down as he was leading another charge at the edge of the airfield. He was posthumously awarded the Navy Cross.

John Basilone did not have to be at Iwo. He had gone the extra mile—for his fellow Marines, and for his country.

GOING THE EXTRA MILE
QUOTES WORTH REPEATING

"You may have to fight a battle more than once to win it."

—Margaret Thatcher

"Failure is not an option."

—Gene Kranz, Apollo 13 Flight Controller

"Character consists of what you do on the third and fourth tries."

—James A. Michener

"Success is a little like wrestling a gorilla. You don't quit when you're tired. You quit when the gorilla is tired."

—Robert Strauss

"Perseverance is the hard work you do after you get tired of doing the hard work you already did."

—Newt Gingrich

"Courage does not always roar. Sometimes courage is the quiet voice at the end of the day saying, 'I will try again tomorrow.'"

—Mary Anne Radmacher

"Even if you're on the right track, you'll get run over if you just sit there."

—Will Rogers

"It is not enough that we do our best; sometimes we must do what is required."

—Winston Churchill

"Most people never run far enough on their first wind to find out they've got a second."

—William James

"The man who can drive himself further once the effort gets painful is the man who will win."

—Roger Bannister

"'Sorry' don't get it done."

—John Wayne, *Rio Bravo*

"Hard work beats talent when talent fails to work hard."

—Kevin Durant

"The whole idea is to get an edge. Sometimes it takes just a little extra something to get that edge, but you have to have it."

—Don Shula

CHAPTER 5

"MAJOR MALFUNCTIONS"

NOBODY SAID IT WOULD BE EASY

When things go wrong, ask yourself: "Other than bitching and worrying about it, what am I *doing* about it?"

Springtime had come to the English countryside. Flowers were blossoming, and birdsong filled the air. Beyond the open window of the car, emerald sweeps of lawn stretched away from the winding road, past stands of huge old trees and rows of hedges. In the quarter mile we had followed along the driveway from the main road, my driver had stopped twice for us to be admitted electronically through strong, imposing gates. We were entering Childwickbury, the estate and manor Stanley Kubrick had purchased in 1977. His secluded domain was in rural Hertfordshire. Here, in 1986, Stanley and his family continued to enjoy the privacy he craved.

My aching body and anxious thoughts were in great contrast to the beauty that surrounded me. I had walked gingerly when approaching the car, and my hired driver assisted me in settling inside. My busted ribs, all six on one side, were on the mend but reminded me not to do anything foolish and risk re-breaking them. My legs and hips were getting stronger thanks to endless sessions on the treadmill, and my shoulder was operational.

I was ready to begin my comeback, ready to begin working daily with Stanley to improve the *Full Metal Jacket* script so that when I was physically able to resume my duties as Drill Instructor Hartman, we would have every scene squared away to perfection. When we were forced to shut down the production in March after my automobile crash, Stanley and I had vowed to use as much of my recovery time as possible to improve the script. Today, we would begin the job and try to turn what had been a gigantic malfunction into a creative advance.

We worked in Stanley's studio, focused on the script, studying it line by line. We began making changes—rewriting, cutting, adding new lines for Hartman. When Stanley activated the tape recorder and said, "Go for it," I would stand up and become Gunnery Sergeant Hartman, doing the scene the same as I would have as a Drill Instructor. I would go until I ran out of gas. Then I would sit down, and we would resume our talks about the scene. We might go through this sequence three or four times a day, with Stanley running the tape that he would, at the end of the day, turn over to his production secretary to transcribe for us.

To begin one of our early meetings, Stanley asked, "How many pages do you think those scenes we worked on yesterday come to when typed?"

I told him I had no idea.

"Twenty-one pages," Stanley said as he held out a sheaf of typed pages filled with the lines I had acted out the day before—without a script. Obviously, this was far too much material to actually use, but we were able to pick the cream of the crop, so to speak.

Working this way, meeting every day during my healing, we changed our huge malfunction into what Stanley called "a godsend." We turned the recruit-training portion of the script into exactly what Stanley liked and wanted to shoot.

Just as the script was on the mend that spring, so was my body. The six broken ribs reminded me of their condition daily, but they were left to heal on their own. I worked with weights on my shoulder. Meantime, I turned to the treadmill to coax my legs, hips, and plumbing system back to Marine Corps fitness. My self-conducted rehab sessions were as close to torture as I ever want to come, but the ultimate results were worth every stab of pain, every drop of sweat.

In a little over two months, I was ready to take on the obstacle course as a test of my fitness. Enduring a wall of pain, I made it through. Drill Instructor Hartman was back in business. Soon the cameras were rolling as I jogged with the recruits, counting cadence.

Then came the unbelievable: more bad luck.

Ironically, we had no sooner started shooting the recruit scenes when a new malfunction ripped up our schedule. This time the glitch happened when Vince D'Onofrio, Private Pyle, pulled a tendon while on the obstacle course. Vince's legs were under abnormal stress because of the extra seventy pounds he put on to play the role.

Now we were in a new fix. Vince had to be in almost every scene and was nursing a crippling injury.

Damage control came in the form of Stanley figuring out ways to shoot around Vince while his injury healed. He also had Vince on camera in ways that did not require the recruit to be physically active. For instance, in one important scene Vince is sitting on his footlocker, cleaning his rifle. Stanley kept the production moving by deftly improvising the schedule.

Meanwhile, his quest for perfection continued. He was the master of lighting and ambience, and he would not accept a scene as wrapped until he was certain he had captured exactly what he wanted. With many directors, you hear the words, "It's good enough. Let's move on." Never with Stanley. If it wasn't perfect, we shot it again. The gripes of the actors and the threats of the producers were ignored.

Few, if any, directors can get away with such autocratic behavior in filmmaking today, with cost overruns and schedules shot to hell, but Stanley was the exception.

Perhaps the ultimate example of Stanley's attention to detail can be seen in the shots of Private Pyle in the "head" in the climax of the recruit-training portion of the film. Stanley took almost an entire week to light the shot. Every day he shot film of the head lighted in different ways with different tiles and different lenses. This was while we were working on other scenes, but every morning he would shoot the experimental shots. The next morning at 4:30 he would watch the developed film, then come in to the set, make new adjustments to the lighting, and reshoot.

Finally, he achieved the effect you see in the film—the icy blue coldness that heightens the horror.

It was also during the shooting of this scene that Stanley went against my technical advice for the only time during the making of *Full Metal Jacket*. We were close to the finish line, wrapping the movie, when he suddenly decided to shake off what I was telling him.

You might say I failed in my mission. I was there to influence Stanley, to sell him my wares—technical accuracy. I did not get it done in that scene.

I was upset, not only because the scene in question was one of the most important in the film, but also because the error was so blatant. Despite my strong protests,

Stanley went ahead and shot the scene his own way. The result was the only technical mistake in the film. It is still pointed out to me by savvy viewers to this day, and I have to squirm when they ask me why I let it happen.

You might say I failed in my mission. I was there to influence Stanley, to sell him my wares—technical accuracy. I did not get it done in that scene. He just wasn't buying.

The scene was Private Pyle's ultimate confrontation with Private Joker and Drill Instructor Hartman. We see Pyle inserting a magazine into his M14. Two rounds can be seen at the top of the clip. Many viewers believe the scene is inaccurate because the recruit could never have gotten live ammo into the barracks. Not so! We Drill Instructors sometimes found a round hidden in footlockers after the ammo had been smuggled back to the depot from the range. Sometimes we found two rounds, maybe three, but never more.

The real error occurs when Private Joker barks out, "Private Pyle has a full magazine."

Uh-oooh. We're in trouble. There is no way Joker could have seen the magazine was full, even if it had been. He could have only seen the same two rounds at the top of the clip that all viewers saw when Pyle loaded the rifle. I recommended that we drop the "full magazine" reference from the script. Stanley wanted it left in, and he shot the scene that way. Shame on Stanley.

Long before that glitch occurred, back when the Vietnam scenes were in production, Stanley went with my advice on every frame of the film. And I do believe that we got it right. Marine-real. Vietnam-real.

In case you haven't noticed, I'm very proud of the movie to this day, and everything I see and hear about *Full Metal Jacket* tells me I am not alone. I was fortunate enough to receive a 1987 Golden Globe nomination for Best Supporting Actor (I lost to Morgan Freeman). I did win the Boston Film Critics Award for Best Supporting Actor, and Stanley won the group's Best Director Award.

It is not these individual accomplishments that make me so proud of the movie, but the team effort that resulted in such a successful and iconic film. A lot of special talents came together in the making of that film, directed by a true leader, Stanley Kubrick. Instead of doing the usual Vietnam anti-war film, Stanley stuck with his goal of making a realistic training and combat film. These Marines endure hard training aimed at pounding one lesson into their bodies and minds. That lesson says they matter on the battlefield. With their rifles and other weapons, each man is a fighter, capable of inflicting great damage on the enemy. The irony of the film—which Stanley clearly saw and appreciated—is that when they get into combat in Vietnam, they meet an enemy who has learned that same lesson.

There are many different ways the movie could have ended after the sniper scenes. The final shots were discussed at length, and many versions were considered. The one chosen shows the men marching along, singing the Mickey Mouse Club theme. They are celebrating their survival and performance under fire. Then we fade out to the credits and the Rolling Stones singing "Paint It Black."

I wasn't particularly happy with the ending. I didn't hate it, but I didn't love it either. It seems to say the Marines are telling the world this was a Mickey Mouse war—one the government would not allow them to win. The other view of the ending is that it has nothing to do with political controversy about the war. The men are singing an easy, familiar tune because they're glad to still be alive.

You can take your pick on the meaning of the ending.

The young men who formed the core of the movie as recruits aren't so young any more, and they have done well in their chosen professions as actors. As I mentioned before, Vince D'Onofrio has played many successful roles. Matthew Modine continued his successful career in New York and Hollywood. I play celebrity golf sometimes with Adam Baldwin ("Animal Mother"), and he has several movies and television pictures to his credit. (He, by the way, is not related to Alec Baldwin and his acting brothers.) Arliss Howard ("Cowboy") and I made a Western movie together, *You Know My Name*.

Stanley is gone. He died suddenly in 1999 at age sixty-nine before his last movie, *Eyes Wide Shut*, was released amid great controversy. He called me at my home, just before he passed, and said, "Lee, the actors took my movie away from me. I couldn't stop them. They ruined it! Don't even bother to see it."

Deep down, Stanley was an artist. He didn't like confrontation. He didn't traditionally hire big-name actors for his films, because he wanted to be able to unquestioningly direct his art *his* way.

The big, powerful actors pushed Stanley around, and he was very vulnerable to that type of power. That very same issue had tormented him on past films as well.

Stanley and I dealt with our share of major malfunctions back in our day. In the end, he ran up against one that even he could not correct.

"What is your major malfunction?" That's the expression Drill Instructor Hartman used when he confronted the emotionally disturbed Private Pyle in a key scene in *Full Metal Jacket*.

> **Nobody wants to hear all the crying, whining, moaning, bitching, complaining, hand-wringing bullshit. It doesn't do a damn bit of a good, and no one respects a whiner!**

The Private was indeed experiencing a "major malfunction" mentally, one that led to tragedy in the film.

In the real Marines, Pyle would have received help. He would have been sent to see the "talking doctors" at Building 410. That's where the Navy professionals worked on the recruits who seemed to be screwed up in the head to try to bring them along. I explained all that to Stanley, and he fully understood. But if we sent Private Pyle to Building 410, we wouldn't have had a movie.

Everyday malfunctions don't usually lead to tragedy, but they can sure as hell mess up your life. Some people cope with them immediately; others sit around cursing their bad luck, waiting for some kind of miracle to pull them out of the shit.

Knock it off!

Nobody wants to hear all the crying, whining, moaning, bitching, complaining, hand-wringing bullshit. It doesn't do a damn bit of good, and no one respects a whiner!

Listen to the voice of Gene Kranz, Apollo 13 flight controller, as portrayed by Ed Harris in the movie *Apollo 13* in the scene after the spacecraft has reported a mission-crippling explosion:

"Quiet down! Quiet down! … Let's work the problem, people."

Work the problem!

The answer to whatever dilemma you're facing is in those words. Whatever major malfunction is tormenting you, whether it's in your head or it's some piece of broken machinery or technology, you must face the situation with calm, deliberate action. You will find help if you need it. You will kick the malfunction in the ass and move on.

If you do not grasp the fact that you are capable of doing this, you are going to be set back time and again by life's booby traps and plain old bad breaks. The problems—the malfunctions—should not throw your train off the tracks or wreck your missions and objectives. You might be delayed while you work on the pain-in-the-butt problem, but you've got to get it done and get back on schedule.

When I returned to the States after my work in *Full Metal Jacket* was completed, I realized that I was not squared away professionally. Until the movie was released and the promotional gears started grinding, I was still a nobody. Character actors with only four movies to their credit are a dime a dozen in Hollywood. I had to go there and start knocking down doors to get the attention of power players who had not yet seen *Full Metal Jacket*. That meant schmoozing and hanging out at every function and party where I could get in the door. It also meant that I was obliged to acquire an agent.

The best agents hold the keys to the kingdom of the acting world. They get your photographs, tapes, and history into the hands of people who are running auditions for parts in new movies. When things click, you get called for an audition. If they don't click, as time goes by, you become shop-worn, no longer the exciting new toy the agency had first signed. They have other exciting new toys now. So you end up having to fire that agent and find another, in spite of the old Hollywood bromide: "Changing agents is like changing deck chairs on the *Titanic*."

I had major malfunctions with a few agents over the years before finally ending up in the capable hands of my manager, Bill Rogin, who has now been my representative for twenty-two years. He graciously consented to write the foreword for this book.

Still, agents can't do it all. Actors still need their own insider contacts, people who can get them to the head of the line with a phone call. That's what happened after I worked with Sidney J. Furie on *The Boys in Company C* and *Purple Hearts*. Sidney is actually the director who first discovered The Gunny—the ultimate Drill Instructor, so to speak. It was his recommendation to Stanley Kubrick that helped put me into *Full Metal Jacket*, my fourth international film.

Now, as I worked to land my first big role after completing *Full Metal Jacket*, Stanley Kubrick came through for me with a phone call to Alan Parker, who was directing a major feature film called *Mississippi Burning*, with Willem Dafoe and Gene Hackman. Parker got in touch with us, and I got the part, my first playing a civilian, Mayor Tilman. The weeks of the shoot were especially interesting for many reasons, but in particular I enjoyed working with Gene Hackman, a brother Marine of four and a half years' service.

In 1988 I was back in front of the cameras as a Marine, this time in another big Vietnam feature, *The Siege of Firebase Gloria*, directed by Brian Trenchard-Smith, a talented Australian. The film is one of my personal favorites, and in my opinion it has never received the attention it deserves.

I was determined not to let my movie career falter after *The Siege of Firebase Gloria*. I had established some decent momentum, with respectable credits and performances to my record, but I knew that only hard work and professionalism would keep me in the game. Even though I was perhaps the only actor in Hollywood who had never had an acting lesson or drama coach, I still showed up for every audition with the confidence that I was going to get the part. I knew my lines backward and forward, and I practiced my interpretation of the role. When I didn't get the part, I tried to study what went wrong, to learn from my mistakes.

Today, I can look back on a variety of roles I played in seventy-five feature and made-for-television movies. In addition to those already mentioned, I portrayed a blacksmith in *Sommersby*, a sheriff in *Switchback*, a gay high school football coach in *Saving Silverman*, a country sheriff in *The Texas Chainsaw Massacre* (2003), a vengeful father in *Dead Man Walking*, a mean boss in *Willard*, and so many others that listing them would put you to sleep.

Each film presented a different challenge, bringing a different person to life on the screen. I have enjoyed my chosen profession immensely, and I have been fortunate in being exactly what every actor longs to be: busy!

In the meantime, Camp Pendleton and the Marine Corps Recruit Depot are not very far down the road in San Diego. When I need to take a break from the smog of "Hollyweird," they are my escape hatch.

Down there, I don't have to be an actor.

I'm a Marine, coming home to hang with the troops.

GUNNY'S RULES FOR
OVERCOMING MAJOR MALFUNCTIONS

◼ THE BEST "MALFUNCTION" ADVICE EVER

I can't recall anybody ever telling me life was going to be easy. I bet you're exactly the same.

Life isn't like a baseball game where your opponent walks the bases full, then walks the winning run across the plate. You've got to get some hits and run the bases. And when you go back on the field, you've got to make some plays.

You don't have to beg, "Put me in, coach!" to get into the game: you're in it already. Now I'm urging you to go out there and try your best, get your hands dirty.

Surrendering—a word that does not exist in the Marine lexicon— to the current difficulties is the worst kind of cop-out. Your problem will only get worse.

The other day I was reminded of that when I came upon a disabled car smack in the middle of the right lane, without flasher lights or even brake lights showing. I stopped my truck behind the car, put on my flashers, and cautiously approached, watching for traffic. The lady inside looked at me, crying, both hands waving in the air in panic. I helped her get the flashers on and used my cell phone to call for aid, then pushed the car to the curb.

For sure, having your vehicle conk out on you is no picnic, but by remaining calm, getting those flashers going, and trying to pull to the side, you might prevent a bad accident. It's all elementary stuff, but when your mind malfunctions and shuts down in panic, bad things can happen.

The next time some malfunction is blocking your path, try to remember the advice of Gene Kranz: "Let's stay cool, people.... Work the problem."

✪ THE BEST CLICHÉ OF THEM ALL

You know why clichés never die? It's because they represent truth.

One of my favorites is, "There's no use crying over spilt milk."

When things go against you, learn from the experience, tighten up the ship, and move on.

✪ OUR PROBLEM-FREE KIDS: WIMPS!

I'm saddened to say that a couple of my friends who coach little kids in soccer and baseball have told me the games are set up so nobody really loses. "You've got to make all the kids feel like winners," we're told.

Come again? How can these kids learn the true meaning of winning without overcoming difficulties, coming from behind, and beating a better team? The caretakers of the Nanny State seem dedicated to turning our kids into wimps. For it is wimps they will become when they start meeting real-life crises that seem crushing and insurmountable. Instead of learning at a very tender age that winning is achieved by superior play—that if you snooze, you lose—they will miss that point entirely. Why work hard if being number one means nothing? Their sports contests become one more classroom, with equality for all. No losers, no winners.

When these kids start getting older, it is inevitable that they will discover that the Nannies have not prepared them for getting smashed in the face. Some of them will rise above that condition and go on to become winners. Others will surrender and merely go along to get along. *Welfare, food stamps, what's the use?* Wimps! Where's their motivation?

✪ MOTIVATION MALFUNCTION: THE ARMY'S BLACK BERET

Berets don't make elite soldiers—Drill Sergeants and hard challenges do.

Small children aren't the only individuals who can't be motivated and trained to overcome extreme difficulties by rigging the game.

Misguided motivational efforts reached high levels back in 2001 when the U.S. Army decided that the wearing of a beret as standard headgear would make all soldiers feel as motivated as the real "Green Beret" troops, the Special Forces. The Green Berets, who had earned their headgear, did not appreciate the "sharing" of beret status. The black beret itself was hot, had no visor, and was generally disliked by soldiers. The whole idea was dumped in 2011 when the Army went to camouflage patrol caps, like baseball caps, as standard headgear when wearing combat fatigues. The black beret is still around, however, and is worn with the Army's service uniform, or dress uniform, at formal events. But we can assume the lesson was learned: berets don't make elite soldiers—Drill Sergeants and hard challenges do.

OVERCOMING MAJOR MALFUNCTIONS
QUOTES WORTH REPEATING

"It's not the first mistake that kills you. It's the second mistake that you make because you're still thinking about the first mistake."

—Bobby Fischer, chess champion

"To be brave in misfortune is to be worthy of manhood; to be wise in misfortune is to conquer fate."

—Agnes Repplier

"One's objective should be to get it right, get it out, and get it over. You see, your problem won't improve with age."

—Warren Buffett

"Determine the thing that can and shall be done, and then we shall find the way."

—Abraham Lincoln

"The problem is not to find the answer, it's to face the answer."

—Terence McKenna

"A problem well stated is a problem half solved."

—Charles Franklin Kettering

"Happiness is not the absence of problems, it's the ability to deal with them."

—Steve Maraboli

"Have you got a problem? Do what you can where you are with what you've got."

—Theodore Roosevelt

"Most people spend more time and energy going around problems than in trying to solve them."

—Henry Ford

"In the final analysis, the questions of why bad things happen to good people transmutes itself into some very different questions, no longer asking why something happened, but asking how we will respond, what we intend to do now that it happened."

—Harold S. Kushner

"All problems become smaller if you don't dodge them, but confront them."

—Admiral William F. Halsey

"For every complex problem, there is a solution that is simple, neat, and wrong."

—H. L. Menken

"There is no such thing as a problem without a gift for you in its hands. You seek problems because you need their gifts."

—Richard Bach

"He has not learned the lesson of life who does not every day surmount a fear."

—Ralph Waldo Emerson

"The problem is not that there are problems. The problem is expecting otherwise and thinking that having problems is a problem."

—Theodore Rubin

"The measure of success is not whether you have a tough problem to deal with, but whether it is the same problem you had last year."

—John Foster Dulles

"Make small commitments and keep them. Be a light, not a judge. Be a model, not a critic. Be part of the

solution, not part of the problem."

—Stephen R. Covey

"The man who has no more problems to solve is out of the game."

—Elbert Hubbard

"To solve any problem, here are three questions to ask yourself: First, what could I do? Second, what could I read? And third, who could I ask?"

—Jim Rohn

"A sad soul can kill you quicker, far quicker, than a germ."

—John Steinbeck

"People don't ever seem to realize that doing what's right's no guarantee against misfortune."

—William McFee

CHAPTER

HARD CORPS

FROM MAGGOT TO MANHOOD

How the Marine Corps shaped a dumb, skinny Kansas farm boy into a veteran who would strive to become their proudest spokesperson.

I t is black-dark at zero four forty-five in most of the world.

Not inside the Marine Corps Recruit Depot billet at San Diego, where I am assigned to begin my aspiring Marine Corps career in April 1961.

At zero four forty-five the overhead lights come on like indoor sunshine, to the accompaniment of a bugle blaring out the call of "Reveille" on a recording. As if this is not sufficient to bring tired young men out of a coma-like sleep, the razor-sharp voice of a Drill Instructor—not recorded!—completes the job. The DI is showered, shaved, dressed, and ready to kick butt at zero four forty-five.

"Move it!" he shouts. "Drop your cocks and grab your socks! Be on the road in two minutes."

The sounds of bedding and clothing being rustled by the recruits are mixed with their occasional expletives, more groaned than shouted.

Then come more commands: "Keep quiet, goddamn it. On the road. Move it, or I'll kick you in the ass so hard your nose will bleed!"

From now until lights out at twenty-one thirty, the DIs will not tolerate conversation or lagging behind. The penalty for either one will put you in a world of hurt. (Ever wonder how many push-ups you can do? You'll find out, many times.)

Formation takes place on the road outside our billet, regardless of weather. It does rain occasionally in the San Diego area. When it does, ponchos draped over us recruits are meant to keep us dry but are not as effective as the sharp-looking raincoats and Smokey Bear covers of the DIs.

When the platoon of seventy men is lined up to the satisfaction of our masters, we are marched to the head, where we are hustled inside in shifts. There are not enough toilets for seventy men at once. The call for urgency keeps coming: "Two minutes. Get it done and wash your frigging hands. Move it!"

If you are in the last shift, the smell in the head can be horrendous. You move on without letting it bother you. There are worse things in the world.

Showers, shaves, and brushing teeth all took place the night before—again in shifts. When the DIs thought they heard talking or the group was moving too slow, they would turn off the hot water. "Maybe a cold shower will get your sorry butts moving!"

Back in the morning formation, the pre-breakfast run begins, with three miles of boots thumping and cadence being called:

One, two, three, four . . .
I love the Marine Corps.

The cadences, most of them R-rated by movie standards, become familiar after a couple of weeks. The voices of our platoon roll them out like exhalations, and the truth is that they make the run go quicker.

Morning chow is next—more lines, more shifts, more DI commands, but good grub. It was damn good after a three-mile run and ahead of the kinds of days we had ahead of us. No doubt about it: the three chow times were the best times of day in Marine Corps Recruit Training.

After morning chow, drills and training come in endless waves throughout the day and into the evening. Except for the harsh shouts of the DIs, who have a seemingly bottomless well of creative expletives, the drills flow past with a kind of sameness. The training sessions, however, are more interesting, demanding attention. In the Marine view, what you learn here may keep you—and the other Marines who are with you—alive some day.

Sometimes our day might be interrupted by a recruit professing to be sick or injured. Sick bay was a fairly big deal, not to be approached with whims like mild headaches. Being admitted to sick bay required DI permission. Then the recruit had to place all his possessions in his seabag and leave it in the DI's quarters while he jogged over to the sick bay for examination. If the recruit was admitted to sick bay, his seabag went with him, since it was unknown when he would be returning to duty.

If a sick bay request was for some minor grievance, the conversation with the DI would go something like this:

"Permission to speak to the Drill Instructor, sir."

"Go ahead, Private."

"Request to go to sick bay, sir."

"What's the problem, Private?"

"Painful blister on my hand, sir."

"Let me see it."

The DI would study the outstretched hand. "Bullshit! I've had worse blisters than that on my dick. Put a Band-Aid on it and get back in formation."

Thus would end one recruit's bid to sit out the day's activities.

In the early weeks of our training, we were called "TURDs"—Trainees Undergoing Recruit Discipline. TURDs were required to leave the top button of their shirts fastened at all times, making it obvious to everybody on the base that they were brand-new maggots.

Hot damn! This was a huge reward. We were no longer FNGs.

This particular maggot, barely seventeen years old at the time, was learning to go with the flow of discipline, drills, and training. I was a strong farm boy, physical and tough. I practically danced over the obstacle course. At about four weeks into the program, I could feel both my body and my mind hardening on attaining my objective—to become a Marine. The DIs could throw all the shit they wanted at me—head-cleaning duty, KP, extra push-ups and pull-ups, tongue-lashings—I held my course and stayed focused.

The day finally came when we were marching in formation and the DI suddenly yelled, "Halt!"

His next command was, "Reach with your right hand and unbutton your top button."

Hot damn! This was a huge reward. We were no longer FNGs, "fucking new guys." (That same expression would later become well used in Vietnam, where all replacements would be known as FNGs.)

It was more or less the eighth week when you could feel that the recruits of our platoon were melding into cohesive proficiency, like a smooth-running machine. We weren't constantly getting our asses chewed out. We had figured out how things had to be done to keep the DIs satisfied.

It was at this same time that I received my first compliment from a DI, or as close to a compliment as you'll ever get as a TURD. We were leaving the rifle range, where I felt very comfortable with my M1 Garand. The DI was even smiling as he said, "Damn, Ermey. Maybe you're not as fucked up as I thought you were."

I guess he was right, because at the end of twelve weeks' recruit training, my platoon was marched to the cattle cars set to haul us to the Infantry Training Regiment at Camp Pendleton. As we left the Recruit Depot behind, six or seven guys from our group were promoted to Private First Class. I was not one of the elite few, but, like my Marine recruit brothers, I was no longer a TURD. We were all heading for four weeks of intense infantry training. This was the stuff I had been waiting for: blowing things up, learning to fight the enemies of our country, becoming a grunt.

All Marines are expected to be combat riflemen regardless of their duty assignment. Infantry training drilled that message into us with great force. Our rifles, our grenades, our combat formations and tactics—they would be the key to victory when the fight came. And we would damn sure be ready!

At boot camp graduation time, I felt as proud and strong as I ever had in my life. I had accomplished my mission: I was a Marine!

Now came twenty days' leave before I was due to report back to the Marine Corps Recruit Depot for sea school. I had volunteered for sea duty and had been selected. The Navy recruiters had turned me down back when I tried to join up, but now I had outfoxed them. I would be going to sea with them anyway.

As I left the base to go on leave, I was checked out by a Staff NCO to make sure my appearance was squared away, Marine style. Civilian clothes had to be well-pressed slacks and shirt; no Levi's or jeans of any type were permitted. Shoes had to be mirror-polished and our haircuts, perfect. The NCO even checked our fingernails. Even going off duty, Marines were expected to look like Marines. If you failed any of these inspections at the gate, you were sent back to your billet to get squared away.

Rather than aggravate me, these last inspections strengthened a powerful notion that had been building inside me. Over the previous several weeks, I had forged my way into a brotherhood. I was no longer alone, a lost, hopeless, and frightened teenager. I was a Marine, part of a team. There were team standards I was expected to meet, and I felt I would almost rather die than screw up and lose my place in these ranks. I had no idea what the future held, but my new position in life filled me with hope. And for the first time ever, I felt the reward of achievement.

At home my dad was especially thrilled by his Marine son's upcoming sea duty. He was a veteran squid, a sailor, who had served aboard a destroyer during World War II. Our conversations about life at sea primed the pump of my anticipation. The Navy's rejection of my service months before still irked me, since I had wanted to follow in the footsteps of my father, so I was doubly ready to make the most of this new opportunity to get on board a ship.

At the eight-week sea school, I quickly learned that the Marine detachments aboard ships were expected to maintain the ultimate spit-and-polish conditions. The sea school NCOs worked our butts off, with inspections every day. Seagoing Marines were under the gaze of a ship's sailors 24/7, and the pressure was intense to not only perform at the highest levels but to look A.J. Squared Away.

Marine detachments had been going to sea on Navy ships since 1775, when the Corps was formed to help fight in the Revolutionary War. It was later tasked with fighting nineteenth-century pirates—specifically, to repel boarders. When my detachment took our station on the USS *Coral Sea* in 1961, our duties were far more complex than those early war fighters could have imagined.

We guarded "weapons spaces," including armed aircraft and weapons aboard the ship. We ran the brig. We lived in our own quarters and were self-sufficient—laundry, chow, everything we needed. We did not spread ourselves among the sailors, but were our own unit. We had our own commanding officer, executive officer, and first Sergeant.

Back then, there were about fifty or sixty such Marine detachments aboard Navy vessels like cruisers and aircraft carriers. Now there are none. The Navy has decided it can handle those duties on its own.

Private R. Lee Ermey, originally from the Kansas prairies, who had never even seen the ocean until he arrived at the Marine Corps Recruit Depot in San Diego, was destined to spend his next two years on an aircraft carrier at sea, patrolling with F4 Phantoms and lots of helicopters. We had aircraft going day and night. I quickly learned why the flight deck of an aircraft carrier was called "the most dangerous football field on earth."

The USS *Coral Sea*, CVA-43, made two Far East deployments, each six months long, while I was on board. We would go out from the West Coast, stop at Hawaii, then on into the Pacific to relieve our sister ship that had been on duty.

Resupply stops were made in the Philippines, Okinawa, Japan, and Guam. Liberty passes were issued, and PFC Ermey began to see parts of the world he had dreamed of visiting back when he had visions of joining the Navy. Sometimes we resupplied at sea, and it was always exciting when the supply ship pulled alongside and started firing lines over to us.

Our carrier patrolled off Vietnam, and we were part of the blockade during the Cuban Missile Crisis of 1962, when the United States and Soviet Union were "eyeball to eyeball" at a time when nuclear war was threatening.

Eventually, after two years of sea duty, I decided it was time to get back to my grunts at Camp Pendleton. I was assigned to the 1st Marine Division.

The Marines gave me what I wanted at Camp Pendleton: endless training sessions, humping it in the field, and preparing for combat operations. I was a Lance Corporal now, with the infantry MOS (military occupational specialty) 0311: rifleman, grunt.

My grunt duties now placed one of the service's most legendary weapons into my hands—the Browning Automatic Rifle. A bulwark of small-unit firepower in World War II and Korea, the BAR had seen better days, but, what the hell, as long as I could keep mine firing, I could take out big numbers of the enemy. I trained to do exactly that, as BARman in the First Fireteam in the First Squad. There were three fireteams in a squad, each team with a fireteam leader, a rifleman, a BARman, and an assistant BARman.

With its fast magazine changes, the BAR could spew out "marching fire," a line of deadly .30-06 caliber rounds raking across the landscape. I loved having that firepower in my hands, but, like all BARmen, I was frustrated by the aging weapon's malfunctions. The BARs we had were so old they rattled when we shook them. When the BAR failed to fire, the immediate standard procedure was *pull, push, tap, aim, and attempt to fire*: pull the operating rod handle to the rear, push it forward, tap the bottom of the magazine, aim, and attempt to fire. Sometimes it worked; often it didn't—a hell of a situation to be in if you were being overrun.

The BAR deserved the reputation it had at that time as the most useless weapon in the Marine Corps. Like all great fighters, the BAR had seen its prime come and go. It was being phased out for the M60 machine gun as the services switched to the 7.62 mm NATO cartridge. The M14 rifle had replaced the M1 Garand in the same cartridge replacement.

Infantry training in the Marines is a never-ending operation, with classes on weapons management, communications, and navigation in the bush. You have to know simple skills like hand signals and more advanced ones like how to read a map, work a compass, and shoot an azimuth. (Remember "Cowboy" in *Full Metal Jacket*? Thrust into command by events, he got his men lost. It was ugly!)

During infantry training, we made patrols and bivouacked for a week at times. We learned how to set up a defensive perimeter, string wire, use Claymore mines, and position foxholes and machine-gun nests. At the combat operations training base in the desert of California, 29 Palms, we trained in working with airplanes and helicopters, calling in air strikes. The physical training was intense, with the obstacle course supplemented by long runs, sometimes in the sand. I took to it all like a duck to water. I was becoming the Marine I thought I should be, a grunt ready for orders to get into a fight.

I was promoted to Corporal, and my time for reenlistment came. Now I took time to reconsider my options. Continuing as an infantry-man did not seem to offer the advancement opportunities I felt I needed. I had joined the Marine Corps for the long haul, and promotions had to be part of that goal. The Marine Corps does not hand out promotions simply because you've put in time at a certain grade. Promotions are earned by doing the hard jobs with 120 percent effort. I was looking over the landscape of opportunities when a visiting group of Staff NCOs and officers told me the Drill Instructor School was looking for volunteers.

There were conditions for admission to DI School: your record would have to be faultless, you would have to survive intense and difficult training, and you would have to be approved by a board. To me, it all sounded like the kind of niche I was looking for, with advancement possibilities. I volunteered for the Drill Instructor School.

My life had come to another game changer. I didn't know it yet, but my Marine Corps duties forevermore would be as a Drill Instructor or training NCO. You might say that the Marine Corps and R. Lee Ermey had both found the perfect fit.

I'm proud to say that I graduated from the Drill Instructor School after eight long, hard weeks and then was approved by the board. I pulled on my Smokey cover for the first time among recruits and went to bird-dog a platoon in training—to watch the DIs in action and get the feel of the operation with India Company, 3rd Battalion, Marine Corps Recruit Depot at San Diego.

On the film set of *The Siege of Firebase Gloria* while shooting in the Philippines.

My dad's Navy boot camp photo.

My mom with her four remaining sons in 1990. Left to right: Terry, Jack, me, and Steve. Since this was taken, she and Steve have passed.

This is the entire family. Boys from left to right: Ed, me, Jack, Mike, Steve, and Terry in Mom's arms.

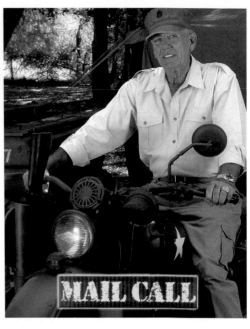

Me on the set of the History Channel's *Mail Call*, season 2006–2007.

Platoon 373's boot camp graduation photo. DIs left to right: Sergeant Payne, Sergeant Tally, and me. This was my second platoon.

This 1989 photo was taken on the set of *The Siege of Firebase Gloria* in the Philippines. The person in the center is Tom Madden, USN (Ret.).

In 1987, *People* magazine wanted this shot of my then young family. Left to right: Betty, Evonne, and Clinton. They are all over thirty now.

On the set of *Full Metal Jacket*, 1986.

Sea Duty aboard the USS *Coral Sea* (CVA-43). Back in the day, Marines wore leather and brass, and all needed to be shined daily.

My dad and me, taken in the '80s. I'm the one on the left.

Recent photo of me on my Victory Highball. This photo was taken in my trophy room.

This old bird can still pick 'em up and set 'em down.

On the deck to my front with the horns and big fur coat lies Tuffy, the best damned bison burger ever. Tuffy was old and beaten by one of the young bulls and had been exiled from the herd. He would have been mountain lion chow, so I beat the lions to him in 2011.

This movie sucked. I refuse to remember the title of it. But it's a great photo!

Here is another graduating recruit platoon. My fellow DIs are Sergeant Sykes and Sergeant Mares.

At the age of twenty, I was one motivated, squared away, hard chargin' Marine Drill Instructor. The youngest in 3rd Battalion.

This is my boot camp photo at seventeen years of age. Was I or was I not one very handsome Devil Dog?

This is what's left of my little VW Rabbit after taking on a walnut tree in Epping Forest. I was hurt badly, but the tree was D.E.A.D. So...I'm the winner!

This was a scale mock-up of our Marine base in *Full Metal Jacket*. Kubrick used these models to work out his camera positions or make changes to the set.

Here is the Master, Stanley Kubrick, on his set calling the shots.

This is the completed version of the mock-up Marine base for *Full Metal Jacket*. No such gate ever existed in Da Nang, but it sure looked great in the movie.

I have always been a firm believer that if it's worth saying, then it should be said loud enough to be heard by all. Sound off like ya gotta pair!

On the obstacle course, this is known as the Stairway to Heaven. Private Pyle was scripted to make it over this obstacle but when the actor got to the top, he panicked due to his fear of heights. In the moment, the script went out the window and I coaxed him down as I would have any recruit. Sometimes the real stuff that happens on the set just can't be wasted.

We're all winners at the NRA National Police Shooting Championships in New Mexico. I'm there every year. Grow some nads, come on down, and see if you pack the gear.

Me speaking at the NRA National Police Shooting Championships.

When I was assigned as third Drill Instructor for a platoon (each platoon had three DIs) in 1965, the demands of the Vietnam War were sending a flood tide of recruits our way. Our normal platoon size of seventy surged to one hundred. Our depot was responsible for the western part of the United States; Parris Island, South Carolina, handled the east.

The sheer number of recruits arriving for training was almost overwhelming in '65. We became so crowded we had recruits living in tents set up on the training fields. Training was cut from twelve weeks to eight.

> **We had no officer supervision. Mostly we ran our own show, training the way we thought best. Things got a little rough once in a while.**

We DIs faced a formidable task. These recruits had eight weeks to learn what we had been teaching in twelve. They were going to Vietnam; we had to get them ready, whatever it took. We weren't afraid of the responsibility. We were trained and ready to take on the job of turning young men into fighting Marines. They had all volunteered; so had we DIs. Now the lives of these men depended on them listening to what we were trying to teach them.

The DIs had been getting six to eight days off between graduating a platoon and picking up a new one. That came to a screeching halt. Things reached the point where we would be picking up a new platoon three or four days before we had even graduated the current batch.

We had no officer supervision. The officers were all in Vietnam, fighting the war. We had some very senior NCOs as staff supervision, but mostly we ran our own show, training the way we thought best. Things got a little rough once in a while with eight weeks instead of twelve. We felt like cutting corners sometimes. Instead of standing there watching a malfunctioning kid do twenty-five sit-ups, we'd give him a shot in the solar plexus and some ass-chewing, and he'd be back in action in two minutes.

After thirty months as a Drill Instructor at San Diego, I finally got orders sending me overseas—but not to Vietnam, into the shit, as I expected. I was destined to spend the next six months on Okinawa, where my aircraft carrier, the *Coral Sea*, had called when I was on sea duty. I continued to train troops there, in one of the loveliest Marine stations on earth, while anticipating the day when I would be sent closer to the fighting.

After six months among the palms and beaches, orders for West-Pac (Vietnam) did arrive. A short time later, I found myself getting off the plane in Da Nang. Finally, I was boots-on-ground in Vietnam.

I arrived just as all hell was breaking loose. The Tet Offensive was slamming into South Vietnam.

It was February 1968. Our nation's weak-kneed leaders had agreed to a cease-fire during January for Tet celebrations, which were like Thanksgiving, Christmas, and New Year's all rolled into one. The NVA had been close to surrender when we gave them the month off. Our forces didn't even leave their bases, while the NVA said, "Look at these stupid Americans." The NVA used the lull to build up their forces. On January 30, with the cease-fire still in effect, they launched surprise attacks on multiple fronts, with some eighty thousand troops. In cities like Hue, they massacred civilians by the thousands. Although the initial attacks shocked U.S. and Vietnamese forces, the NVA was beaten back within weeks with horrendous losses to their armies. The left-wing press establishment seized Tet to ramp up their chant that the war was not only unnecessary, but was going badly. They succeeded in keeping our already-wavering leaders on the defensive and actually had the American public believing we had lost the war, which was total bullshit.

At Da Nang, despite things blowing up all around the base, my assignment did not thrust me into the frontline fight. Because of NCO scuttlebutt, my reputation as a DI had preceded me. I was no sooner off the plane than a Gunnery Sergeant from the 1st Marine Air Wing grabbed my ass. I was assigned to the 1st MAW as their training NCO.

My duties were to supervise the training for the Marine Wing, Support Group 17. In addition I was put in charge of the Immediate Reaction Platoon that was assigned to man the perimeters of the base during attacks. If rockets were falling, we hit the bunkers until we could move out to our foxholes and trenches at the wire. Then we had two minutes to get into position. We trained hard and were ready to go 24/7.

Troops being trained in 1st MAW had jobs in keeping aircraft flying and shooting—maintenance, rocket loading, and a variety of other technical skills. Of course, they all had gone through infantry training and knew what to do with weapons in their hands. We had regular infantry troops to train as well, and I worked with them in drills and classes at the base, and took them on MEDCAP (medical civil action program) missions to small villages in nearby Happy Valley.

I was a Staff Sergeant now, and the challenges for me were a lot different from wet-nursing a platoon of boot camp recruits. But I was still training troops. Training … training … day after day … a lot of "hurry up and wait" time … the heat like a physical blow … many faces passing before me, then moving on … time itself slowly moving on.

On a base under rocket attack from time to time, I wasn't exactly "in the rear with the gear," as some Marines describe certain posts. Nevertheless, I yearned to spend more time outside the wire, closer to the shit, as they say.

When I had time off from training troops, I volunteered for resupply duties. In our helicopters, I began visiting all the I Corps Firebases, helping the crews resupply ammo, C-rations, water, beer—whatever the bases needed. From the Rockpile to Camp Carroll, I think I got in at least one trip to most I Corps Firebases.

My Vietnam experience came to a close after sixteen months, when orders sent me back to the friendly Marine posts at Okinawa. Training troops beside the beaches was quite different from the sauna that was Vietnam, and I welcomed the change. In particular, I enjoyed snorkeling on my days off. Life on Okinawa was like another world compared with Vietnam. It would have been perfect except for my shoulder that had been injured in a rocket attack at Da Nang. I kept quiet about it, popping it back into place from time to time, but it was becoming an issue.

When I received orders to leave Okinawa for new duties training troops at the Marine Air Wing, Cherry Point, North Carolina, I paid a visit to my folks in Washington state. I had heard rumors about returning Vietnam veterans being treated with shameful disrespect in San Francisco and other large cities, but I expected no such harassment when I wore my uniform back home. This was small-town, grassroots America, and the folks there did not disappoint me. I couldn't buy a drink or meal for myself while on leave, and the smiles and handshakes were warm and genuine. Good thing, too, for the sake of my service record. If anybody had spit on me like they had on returning troops in San Francisco, they would have eaten a knuckle sandwich.

At Cherry Point, North Carolina, I was training troops and, except for my bad shoulder, life was good. This was 1972, my eleventh year as a Marine, and my sights were still set on a career. As a matter of fact, I even harbored a secret ambition to become Sergeant Major of the Marine Corps some day. Dreaming big was still my style. I call it "setting goals."

One day the Sergeant Major of the Marine Air Wing called me into his office. He wasn't smiling. I sensed bad news coming. Had somebody died at home? I could think of nothing else that would fill the room with such a feeling of gloom.

"Ermey, I'll give it to you straight. You're being transferred to the TDRL, the Temporary Disability Retired List. It's your shoulder. You'll be getting a small pension."

I had suspected the medics were going to get me. The Marines were cutting back on troop numbers. The Corps only had room for the 100 percent fighting fit. Guys like me with bad body parts were being let go, retired. My lifetime career was over in eleven years.

> **My lifetime career was over in eleven years.**

As you have seen in the previous chapters, the Marines didn't yet know that I was going to keep showing up for work.

"Once a Marine, always a Marine," it was said.

Damned straight!

MAGGOT TO MANHOOD
QUOTES WORTH REPEATING

"Some people live an entire lifetime and wonder if they ever made a difference in the world, but the Marines don't have that problem."

—President Ronald Reagan

"Marines I see as two breeds, Rottweilers or Dobermans, because Marines come in two varieties, big and mean, or skinny and mean. They're aggressive on the attack and tenacious on defense. They've got really short hair and they always go for the throat."

—Rear Admiral Jay Stark

"If I charge, follow me. If I retreat, kill me. If I die, revenge me."

—Anonymous Marine

"I'm not scared of very much. I've been hit by lightning and been in the Marine Corps for four years."

—Lee Trevino

"My Marine experience helped shape who I am now personally and professionally, and I am grateful for that on an almost daily basis."

—Jim Lehrer

"The aim of every woman is to be truly integrated into the Corps. She is able and willing to undertake any assignment consonant with Marine Corps needs, and is proudest of all that she has no nickname. She is a Marine."

—Colonel Katherine A. Towle

"There's a mindset of flexibility and adaptability that comes with us. We don't mind hardship. We don't mind somebody saying, 'Go in and do this nasty job.' Whatever the job is, we can do it. That's why the nation has a Marine Corps."

—General James F. Amos

"I have drawn inspiration from the Marine Corps, the Jewish struggle in Palestine and Israel, and the Irish."

—Leon Uris

"There is no better friend, and no worse enemy, than a United States Marine."

—Anonymous

"Teufelhunde! [Devil Dogs!]"
    —German soldiers referring to U.S. Marines during WWI

"The deadliest weapon in the world is a Marine and his rifle!"

—U.S. Army General John J. "Black Jack" Pershing

"They [women Marines] don't have a nickname, and they don't need one. They get their basic training in a Marine atmosphere, at a Marine post. They inherit the traditions of the Marines. They are Marines."

—General Thomas Holcomb

"They say, 'You can lead a horse to water, but you can't make him drink.' In the Marine Corps, you can make that horse wish to hell he had."

—Sergeant Fred Larson, Drill Instructor

"Son, when the Marine Corps wants you to have a wife, you will be issued one."

—Lieutenant General Lewis B. "Chesty" Puller, when asked by a Private for permission to marry

"Old breed? New breed? There's not a damn bit of difference so long as it's the Marine breed."

—Lieutenant General Lewis B. "Chesty" Puller

"And once, by God, I was a Marine."

—Actor Lee Marvin

CHAPTER

THE PRICE OF FREEDOM

THE GUNNY WANTS YOU

Peace can't be guaranteed, because you never know for sure what your enemies might do. But as long as our men and women continue to step forward to serve in our military, we will live in freedom.

I have to think that William Shakespeare would have made one hell of a Drill Instructor.

Listen to him here, for instance, in *Henry V*:

> We few, we happy few, we band of brothers;
> For he today that sheds his blood with me
> Shall be my brother; be he ne'er so vile
> This day shall gentle his condition;
> And gentlemen in England now a-bed
> Shall think themselves accursed they were not here,
> And hold their manhoods cheap whiles any speaks
> That they fought with us upon Saint Crispin's day.

A man who can come up with stuff like that ought to have no problem in holding the attention of recruits.

In my Drill Instructor years, I didn't have much time to win the recruits' attention with war stories. They would have listened to each and every word, of course. But, I was no Shakespeare.

Years after my DI days, however, I began teaching courses in military history. I'm not kidding; I really did! Perhaps you attended a couple of my classes. My credentials for lecturing on the subject were the fire in my gut and the images in my memory. My blackboard was in front of the cameras and held by the crew of the television show *Mail Call*, which aired on the History Channel for eight seasons.

> "Come on, you sons of bitches! Do you want to live forever?" Marine Gunnery Sergeant Dan Daly yelled to his men.

As narrator and host, I took the History Channel's *Mail Call* to as many actual battlefields as I could during the show's original seven-year run. My mission: reminding viewers that freedom is not free.

The History Channel's *Mail Call* covered a variety of subjects on all military branches, ranging from the newest weapons and gear to historic artifacts. My favorite segments were those where our cameras and crew were boots-on-ground in actual places where our men and women in uniform fought battles that should never be forgotten.

We went to Normandy Beach, with its artillery and machine gun emplacements overlooking the sands that our troops had to cross out in the open. In two separate segments we honored those who fought on the lava fields of Iwo Jima where Japanese forces rained down machine-gun, mortar, and artillery fire on the beaches beneath the looming hulk of Mount Suribachi. We showed our audiences the Belleau Wood area in France where Marines first went into battle in World War I. It was there where the Germans gave us the name "Devil Dogs," and Marine Gunnery Sergeant Dan Daly yelled to his men, "Come on, you sons of bitches! Do you want to live forever?"

In Vietnam we visited firebases where being surrounded was an everyday situation. Places like Khe Sanh, Camp Eagle at Phu Bai, the Rockpile, Dong Ha, Marble Mountain, and China Beach. My film crew and I spent an entire day filming at the notorious "Hanoi Hilton" where heroes like John McCain withstood torture. The battlefields where our troops were on duty in Iraq and Afghanistan were still hot when we went there with our cameras and crew.

Here at home, our cameras trained on poignant testaments to the sacrifices of our military personnel: the Vietnam Wall, where it is impossible to find a familiar name without viewing it through tears; the Marine War Memorial where Joe Rosenthal's photograph has been transformed into figures thirty-three feet high in a stunning bronze statue; Arlington Cemetery and the Tomb of the Unknown; the National Museum of the Marine Corps at Quantico; the Pentagon; and many other sites that always bring a lump to my throat.

The History Channel's *Mail Call* was a very popular show back in its day, from 2002 to 2009, and it is still shown in reruns on the Military History Channel.

The truth is that I get downright sentimental when I think about the sacrifices of blood, guts, and sweat by our military personnel over the decades. And I feel very proud when I think about those on duty today, serving our nation. I jump at the chance to talk about them all, whether in front of cameras or at Marine Corps Birthday Balls or other events. And I snap to attention and salute when I hear the first notes of "The Star-Spangled Banner." But don't expect to see The Gunny moved or in any way emotionally pleased when seeing and hearing some rock star or hip-hop singer trying to put their own personal jive twist onto the singing of our national anthem. "The Star-Spangled Banner" needs no special interpretations by self-aggrandizing performers out to put on a show. The standard notes and melody work just fine, and they stir deep feelings within me when I hear them delivered strong and true.

I'm also not amused when the hometown sports crowd starts screaming and drowning out the singer as he or she is trying to deliver the final words. For it is at the conclusion of those words that I believe Francis Scott Key completes his message with a stroke of genius: a question mark.

The last sentence is not a statement. It is a question.

> Oh, say does that star-spangled banner yet wave,
> O'er the land of the free, and the home of the brave?

There you have it: the question every generation of Americans must answer.

When the anthem has ended, and everybody stands down, relaxes, watches the game … whatever…that last sentence still lingers, that burning question remains.

The answer is, "Yes!" Our flag does yet wave, over the land of the free and the home of the brave. And it will continue to do so as long as we have men and women in uniform giving at least some portion of their lives to serve their country.

Many people don't quite understand how totally obligated a young man or woman becomes when signing on the dotted line for military service. It's 24/7 for four years.

You want to do your own thing, you say? Then don't join up!

The personal sacrifices of privacy and individualism that service life requires are not usually noticed by the public or noted by the media. Privacy in the lives of service personnel ranks between very little and none, no matter what you're doing, from brushing your teeth to hitting the sack.

You want privacy? You'll have to wait until you go home on leave. Individualism is lost to the demands of serving your unit—your squad, your platoon, your aircraft, your ship. You exist to serve your unit, your team. That's your world.

You want to do your own thing, you say? Then don't join up! Stay home with mama and let someone who's got a pair pull your share of the load.

Life in the service can be as funny as Andy Griffith in *No Time for Sergeants* or as grim as *Saving Private Ryan*. It's a diverse experience depending on where you're stationed, your job, your mission, your NCOs and officers, and your attitude.

President John F. Kennedy, speaking of calling up reservists in the Berlin Wall crisis, described it this way: "There is always inequity in life. Some men are killed in a war, and some men are wounded, and some men are stationed in the Antarctic and some are stationed in San Francisco. It's very hard in military or personal life to assure complete equality. Life is unfair."

I reckon that by now you know where The Gunny is heading with this speech.

If you're of an age eligible for military service, I want you to consider joining.

Army, Air Force, Navy, Marines—I don't care which branch. Coast Guard, too, but you should be aware that enlistment quotas for the Coast Guard are very small, and getting in is not easy. With current budget cuts you may have to go on a waiting list to get into the other branches as well. And, I'm sorry to have to be the one to tell you if you don't know it already, if you've screwed up your life with drugs and arrests, you're not going to get in.

I used the words "consider joining."

Perhaps you're well on your way to the education and employment niche you feel will make you happy. You're committed to a path that's not easy to leave even though the call for service is not alien to your nature. In peacetime, no one can ever blame you for sticking with your present course.

On the other hand, perhaps you still haven't nailed down the career path, the lifestyle, even the education that might open the door to a future you can anticipate with great enthusiasm. Perhaps you're drifting. There's nothing wrong with you; you're just not sure what you want to do, where you want to be in the long haul.

Could be it's time to talk with a service recruiter. You can tell them what you have to offer—and they can tell you what our armed services have to offer in return. Common military benefits include career skills training, education, interesting assignments, a chance to show leadership and take on heavy responsibilities at a young age, and travel. Perhaps you see yourself as an Army or Marine infantry grunt, training to fight. Maybe you even feel strong enough to be in Special Units, like Navy SEALS, Army Rangers, or Marine Reconaissance.

And even if you're heading into college for four years, ROTC could certainly be a strong option to consider. You'll nail down your education and then serve your country as an officer.

Whatever happens, after four years of service, if you decide to return to civilian life, you'll be far, far better prepared than if you had spent those four years doing things like flippin' burgers. If your service duties have been in the communications field, perhaps you'll find a spot in civilian life in some high-tech operation. If you've been in the infantry or Special Ops for four years, perhaps you'll find an opening in the rapidly growing homeland defense field. If you use them well, four years of military service can open lots of doors when you're looking for a job in civvies. Look where I ended up!

Consider this also: service life might turn out to be just what you were looking for. The military offers a community unlike anything the civilian world can match, in my opinion. I wouldn't be surprised at all if you never wanted to leave. I sure didn't. My injured shoulder forced me out of active duty; I didn't go willingly.

Even after fifty-two years with the Marines, I still feel the unique pull of military service. It's the camaraderie; the different bases around the world; the different missions and the ever-changing weapons and tools that make them possible; and the sense of community and belonging to a team that goes in and wins.

But if four years for you are enough, you can put away your uniform with pride, knowing you have served your country. You will be a veteran, forever in the ranks of so many who have stepped forward to answer Francis Scott Key's question.

GUNNY'S RULES OF ENGAGEMENT
THE PRICE OF FREEDOM

✪ ENLISTMENT INFO AT YOUR FINGERTIPS

You can fast-start your education about military enlistment requirements and what the different services offer at these excellent websites: GoArmy.com; Marines.com; Navy.com; AirForce.com; and GoCoastGuard.com.

✪ BRIEFING PARENTS, THE GUNNY WAY

I've heard this one from time to time: "Gunny, I'm interested in joining up, but my mom and dad are afraid."

Your Gunny suggests that you tell them to do what parents have been doing since Americans first fought at Concord and Lexington in the Revolution: Suck it up!

When they see their sons or daughters in Class A uniforms after their graduation and start receiving letters and emails about their duty assignments, their pride will overcome their fears.

✪ THE DRILL INSTRUCTOR'S CREED

From the moment I first came under the scrutiny of Drill Instructors at the Recruit Training Depot at San Diego, I only knew them as fierce taskmasters ready to kick my butt or throw it off the base—or both! I was too young and dumb to realize that these were men who had a job to do, and that they had made a pledge to the Marines that they would accomplish their mission.

Later, when I was fortunate enough to become a DI myself, the Drill Instructor's Creed became my personal mantra:

These recruits are entrusted to my care. I will train them to the best of my ability. I will develop them into smartly disciplined, physically fit, basically trained Marines, thoroughly indoctrinated in love of Corps and country. I will demand of them, and demonstrate by my own example, the highest standards of personal conduct, morality and professional skill.

> **For the record, many of the women in the Marine ranks could probably kick your wimpy ass!**

★ THE TOUGHEST RECRUIT TRAINING: SEMPER FI!

Sometimes a misguided pilgrim will say to me, "Gunny, the Marines have lots of women in their ranks, like everybody else. Boot camp can't be that tough."

Dude, where've you been? The Marines do not train men and women together in boot camp. All Marine women recruits go to the Women's Recruit Depot at Parris Island, South Carolina. Men from the eastern United States go to the Men's Recruit Depot at Parris Island; from the western United States, they go to the Depot at San Diego.

Not all that much has changed in Marine recruit training since I was a TURD or since I was a Drill Instructor. It's still the toughest out there because, like the man said, "We're not training people to teach Bible school."

And, for the record, many of the women in our ranks could probably kick your wimpy ass!

★ AN ARMED SERVICES UPDATE

This year marks my fifty-second anniversary with the Marine Corps, and obviously I have seen many changes. However, as I tell Marines at the Corps' Birthday Balls that I speak at every November, there is only one fundamental change: today's Marines have more and better toys to play with.

The same goes for the Army, Navy, and Air Force.

Since the days when I lugged a BAR and tried to coax it to shoot, weapons have evolved into powerful, mobile firepower I would have loved to have gotten my hands on in my days of active duty. The communication tools that are commonplace now would have seemed like science fiction fantasy to us back in the sixties.

Back then, a Marine in the bush could be stranded, in need of a medevac, and looking up at an Army helicopter—but would have to go through Army communication channels to direct it to help him and his men. Today, new-age communications and better inter-service cooperation have changed everything. Back then, a letter from home took three weeks to reach Vietnam. By then the girl who wrote you "Dear John" could be singing, "I'm getting married in the morning." Today a soldier or Marine can be communicating with folks at home over his laptop in real time.

Communications, weapons, tactics—it's all a brave new world.

The missions, however, remain the same: to fight and win!

◼ WOMEN IN INFANTRY COMBAT: A BAD IDEA

Women are just as tough as men. I'll agree to that thought. No problem.

Women are as strong as men. Only a complete fool would think that.

Recently, our leaders decreed that women should be allowed to participate in infantry combat if they can qualify. This dumb idea, which is entirely created by the desire to be "politically correct," surfaced back in the early nineties and met immediate resistance from the Marine Corps.

In a dramatic statement, the Twelfth Sergeant Major of the Marine Corps, Harold G. Overstreet, carried a Marine infantry combat pack into the hearing room on Capitol Hill and dropped it. The 120 pounds of gear hit the floor with a big thud. Overstreet challenged any woman in the room to just pick up the gear and walk with it—far less a mission than carrying the pack and equipment ten miles and then fighting with it, as the Marines do. There were no takers.

I'm all for women in the military and for their taking on any roles where they qualify by meeting the same standards as the men (not politically correct—and real-life dangerous—"dual standards"). If a woman can slide into the cockpit of an F-16, handle the g-force, and head for the fight, let her rip.

The fact remains that very few women are strong enough to hump their share of the load in infantry combat. They will have to have help—which creates problems maintaining the integrity, discipline, and effectiveness of the fighting unit.

Now our forces are told that women must be allowed to test for infantry combat. That will require time and manpower in a force that is shrinking, not growing. Already there are questions about whether the politicians intend to shred our military's integrity in order to have the pretty-picture military some of them apparently want. Will standards be lowered? For instance, will women have to simply hang on the pull-up bar while men are required to do a minimum of three pull-ups or go home?

The rigors of infantry combat are real, and right now, even a large percentage of men fail to qualify for combat duty.

I happen to have five daughters, and not one of them has any desire to join infantry combat units. That's true of most women in the military as well.

This entire issue of women in infantry combat is going to waste time and manpower and may eventually result in losses on the battle-field. The Gunny is more than upset about it. I'm pissed!

✪ MILITARY LIFE'S TOUGHEST MILE

When you hear bitching and moaning by troops or officers in military units, it's usually about separation from their families. Missions involving redeployments—and we've had plenty of those since we took on our enemies in Iraq and Afghanistan—take their toll. When husbands and wives are separated by deployment, military families undergo stress loads not seen in civilian life. These aren't like business trips, where mom or dad will be home in a few days. For many months, children and one of their parents must cope with keeping the family unit intact and functioning. It's not easy with mom or dad overseas, but life must go on. This kind of challenge is being faced daily by many American service families, and most of them find a way to make things work until dad or mom comes home.

There are plenty of support groups manned by experienced vet-erans who have lived through separation and are ready to reach out and help those who find it difficult. In the military, we take care of our own. Which is not to say that civilians can't help out. If you know a military family where dad or mom is posted overseas, do the right thing and offer a helping hand, because remember: that's a family that's sacrificing to preserve *your* freedom.

◼ ON BEING A MARINE

I've learned a thing or two about the Marines in my fifty-two years with the Corps.

I still like the truth that resonates from the famous recruiting slogan: THE FEW, THE PROUD, THE MARINES.

Joining their ranks was by far the best thing that R. Lee Ermey ever did.

Semper Fi!

DID YOU COPY?
QUOTES WORTH REPEATING

"Freedom is never more than one generation away from extinction. We didn't pass it to our children in the bloodstream. It must be fought for, protected, and handed on for them to do the same, or one day we will spend our sunset years telling our children and our children's children what it was once like in the United States where men were free."

—Ronald Reagan

"Your instincts are the sum total of your education, experience, reading and training. Listen to your instincts, make the decision and move on. And, always expect the unexpected."

—Lieutenant General Hal G. Moore

"Every good soldier wants to live in an organized environment, secure in the knowledge that he or she will not be threatened or harassed by others, confident that his or her efforts will be recognized, and aware that the nonproductive soldier will be invited to leave. In such an environment, soldiers will be proud of their units and will demonstrate that pride with their performance and behavior."

—Sergeant Major William A. Connelly

"When it's all over and you're home once more, you can thank God that twenty years from now, when you're sitting around the fireside with your grandson on your knee and he asks you what you did in the war, you won't have to shift him to the other knee, cough, and say, 'I shoveled shit in Louisiana.'"

—General George S. Patton Jr.

"You're not being paid by how hard you work, but by what you accomplish. If you can't hack it, pack it. Our challenge today is to look forward, to write our own history."

—Sergeant Major William A. Connelly

"In the beginning of a change, the patriot is a scarce man, and brave, and hated and scorned. When his cause succeeds, the timid join him, for then it costs nothing to be a patriot."

—Mark Twain

"I can imagine no more rewarding a career. And any man who may be asked in this century what he did to make his life worthwhile, I think can respond with a good deal of pride and satisfaction: 'I served in the United States Navy.'"

—President John F. Kennedy

"These are the times that try men's souls. The summer soldier and the sunshine patriot will, in this crisis, shrink from the service of their country; but he that stands it now, deserves the love and thanks of man and woman."

—Thomas Paine

"In the final choice, a soldier's pack is not so heavy a burden as a prisoner's chains."

—President Dwight D. Eisenhower

"Every man thinks meanly of himself for not having been a soldier."

—Samuel Johnson

"This nation will remain the land of the free only so long as it is the home of the brave."

—Elmer Davis

CHAPTER

"POINT MAN"

THE GUNNY'S VIEWS ON LEADERSHIP

Show me you've got a pair by stepping up, taking the reins, and driving the wagon.

U p front, where the action is—that's where you want to be when you're young, fit, and Devil Dog–ready. Spending all your time in the rear with the gear is not very appealing when you could, instead, step up, make your mark, and show the world what you can do.

Have you thought about a leadership role? Are you setting your sights on being in charge of a unit, calling the shots, giving the orders?

If such ambition has crossed your mind, whether in the military or in civilian life, then listen up. The Gunny can help you accomplish the mission of aspiring to leadership.

Great leaders emerge from all walks of life, with personalities as diverse as you can imagine. Their formal education varies from lofty university degrees hanging in gilded frames to high school diplomas tucked away in drawers.

General Douglas MacArthur graduated number one in his class at West Point. President Harry S. Truman was not even a college graduate! Yes, you read that right. Harry S. Truman was the only president in the twentieth century without a college degree.

No two men could have been more different than Douglas MacArthur and Harry Truman, yet they were both true leaders.

General MacArthur was as flamboyant and colorful as they come and was a combat hero in World War I.

President Truman was a quiet, self-effacing son of a Missouri farmer in America's heartland. He served five years in the National Guard, and then when World War I broke out, he volunteered for service at age thirty-three even though he was two years over the draft age and eligible for exemption as a farmer. He rose to the rank of captain in an Army field artillery unit fighting in the Meuse-Argonne, and he served with bravery and distinction.

Immediately, if not sooner, I want you to forget everything you've ever heard about so-called "born leaders." There are no such creatures! They simply don't exist.

Leadership cannot be taught! I can't do it, the Sergeant Major of the Marine Corps can't do it, and instructors at Annapolis, West Point, or the Air Force Academy can't do it. Leadership is not something one "gets." It's something one evolves into.

You heard me. Leaders *evolve*. Most anyone can grow into a leadership role over time through the lessons they learn from their own successes and failures and by observing how others before them acted and reacted in particular situations. Observing how others lead—or fail to lead—is the absolute best classroom for becoming a true leader yourself.

Your chance to motivate others comes as you show them how *you* take on the tasks facing your team. You *show* them that it can be done—and how. You take charge. That's leading by example. With your actions, you inspire and motivate those around you to emulate you. When you lead well, you'll start to realize the people under you and around you will willingly follow you to hell if that's where you're headed. And when that starts to happen, when people back you without question, you'll know you're on your way to becoming a true leader.

True leadership is contagious. Its effects move quickly through the ranks when troops see leaders perform and are inspired to emulate them. When a twenty-one-year-old Marine Sergeant is put in charge of a multi-million-dollar helicopter, it's no accident that he learns how to step into his position by following the examples of leaders he served under.

Somewhere up the road, you might earn a promotion. You will be in charge of the troops. And because you have been a keen observer of true leaders, you will understand that being a boss and giving orders do not make you a leader. Leadership is more than a matter of giving orders and being in charge: it is a matter of character, earned respect, doing the right thing, and always giving your best not only for yourself, but for others. You will become, and remain, committed to demonstrating the leadership qualities you've observed and admired over time.

We all have role models we admire. Even I do!

Personally, I have seen true leaders in action everywhere from forward firebases in Vietnam to offices in the Pentagon. I have seen them in squads on patrol in jungles, in motor pools at a dozen Marine bases, and in billets crammed full of recruits at San Diego. I have seen them in my movie experiences, working with dedicated directors like Stanley Kubrick and Sidney J. Furie.

But, when I think about it, my first and best role models were always my Marine Corps Drill Instructors, Gunnery Sergeant Freestone, Staff Sergeant Sponenberg, and Sergeant Devorak. I was a screw-off, and they knew it.

They recognized my weaknesses and drove them out of me. They screamed and pushed and drove me like I'd never been driven before—or since.

> **When I jaw-jacked instead of listening, they got in my face relentlessly. (I can still see the unique shape of each one of their uvulas wagging in the backs of their throats.)**

When I didn't pay attention during drill, they made me—and those around me—pay with endless push-ups. When I jaw-jacked instead of listening, they got in my face relentlessly. (I can still see the unique shape of each one of their uvulas wagging in the back of their throats.) When I lollygagged on my way getting back into formation after chow, they assigned me step-ups. In fact, I earned so many step-ups that every evening while my fellow recruits were getting ready for the rack, putting an extra shine on their boots, squaring away their foot lockers, or reading letters from home, I was right outside the DI hut trying to work off the step-ups I'd earned. I never did catch up. Hell, I still owe them a few thousand reps!

And I've never forgotten them or the methods they used to mold me into the man I am today.

I learned from each of these men that I could withstand and accomplish and expect more from myself than I'd ever imagined possible. As hard as they were on me, I know it was for a good rea-son—because they recognized the capacity for more from me.

What I didn't realize until I went to DI School myself was that intimidation, fear, and exhaustion were very specific tactics each DI was expected to master; he had to know how and when to deploy them effectively to engage with recruits. The need for mastery of these tactics was not just for the sake of coming off as a hard-ass, but because these are the most effective and efficient and proven methods for tearing an individual down so you can build him back up and teach him to trust his leaders as if his life depended on it, because in combat it will. Instant obedience to orders can mean the difference between mission success or failure, life or death.

This kind of trust must be hard earned to be authentic. And ulti-mately that's what a leader must do—earn the unwavering trust of the people in his command. And that trust is not something that is easily handed over.

Leaders must, of course, master fear, but even more important, they must be knowledgeable—they need to know their business, whatever it is, inside and out. When I entered the Marines, I didn't know much beyond how to take care of a farm (and how to stay out of my father's way when I caused trouble). And my lack of knowledge showed.

In the Marines, junior enlisted personnel usually need a minimum of six months in grade before they can be advanced to the next pay-grades. But there is no guarantee that you'll be promoted just because you're eligible.

After boot camp, I spent nearly two years—twenty-two months, to be exact—at the rank of Private First Class. For a while, I told myself I didn't care, and I continued to carry on like the immature young fool I was. But a second go-round with the shore patrol helped me find my way.

During my first tour, while I was on sea duty, I viewed ship time as nothing more than transportation to the next port where I couldn't wait to get off and find the first bar, get drunk, and pick a fight. Thankfully, though, after a repeat performance or two with shore patrol hauling my sorry butt back to the ship, I landed myself on several months of restriction. It was one of the best things that ever happened to me because it gave me enough time to consider that all that drinking and fighting really wasn't good for me or my career. So, while I was stranded on deck, I figured, "What the hell," and spent my time taking a Marine Corps Institute course in Techniques of Military Instruction.

Now, I had absolutely no thoughts whatsoever of staying in the Marine Corps beyond four years. For me, this MCI course was just a way for me to pass my time on restriction. But it wasn't long before the skills I'd learned from taking the class were noticed by my superiors, and I was appointed the tactical training person on board ship.

As I focused on how to teach and how to better handle my weapon, there finally came a time when I realized that no amount of charm, luck, or time in grade was going to get me promoted. If I wanted to move up, I'd have to earn it.

Who knew this troublemaker's life could be turned around by the decision to take a class and gain knowledge, but that's really what started me on the road to gaining the respect of my superiors. They saw potential. A few months on the good-behavior list got me promoted to Lance Corporal.

I've always believed that what we imitate is what we naturally become. Though I didn't know it at the time, when I took that course, I began emulating leaders before me who sought knowledge as the first step to leadership. If you want to be a drug-dealing criminal, you'll find yourself hanging out with and looking up to drug-dealing criminals to learn how to be one. If you want to be a leader, you'll naturally surround yourself with people who expect more from you.

And you'll take advantage of every chance to gain skill in your job, educate yourself, and earn your way to the top. No leader ever emerged from taking a "that's not my job" attitude, or from shirking hard work, or from not trying to master everything that is required from him.

After I got off the ship and transferred to the 1st Marine Division at Camp Pendleton, I didn't spend much time on liberty in town. I started watching people I worked for who seemed to be earning promotions. They arrived early and stayed late, never leaving until the job was done.

I started hanging back during liberty, studying. I was motivated by friends who were being promoted when I wasn't, and I decided I wanted more reward, more money, but also more responsibility.

Not long after, I heard about the Drill Instructor Board coming around. That sounded like a good opportunity to me. So I prepared for it and worked to earn orders to go to DI School.

I'll always remember the day I stood before a psychiatrist, a senior Staff NCO, and a naval doctor, answering their questions while they reviewed my service record book and scrutinized my awards and merits. When one of them asked me, "What would you do if a recruit spit in your face, Ermey?" and I didn't answer, "Well, I'd punch him in the snot locker, sir," I knew I'd matured. Instead of leading with my typical cocky answer, I said something along the lines of, "I would certainly see that the Private was disciplined," and left it at that. I'd finally learned some self-control, by God, and in this case, it was rewarded with orders to DI School, where I spent eight weeks learning the art of leadership and motivation.

Like most things for me, DI School wasn't a slam dunk. In fact, I almost got kicked out. During my training, I was to give a troop class to my fellow trainees; I chose the topic of safety, care, and cleaning of the M14 rifle.

> **I reached down, pulled the trigger, and unloaded a live blank. A big bang and a lot of smoke filled the classroom.**

I recalled from that Techniques of Military Instruction course I'd taken back on the ship that a good teacher always includes an attention-gainer at the beginning of the class. I needed to come up with a way to walk up to the front and get the focus and undivided attention of one hundred or more people in a hot, crowded classroom.

So, when it was time to teach my class, I walked up to the front of the room, put my rifle upside down on the table with the trigger guard pointing up and the barrel pointing to the right. Then, I called my (prepared) volunteer to the front to assist me. He walked around the right side of the table and started to reach for the weapon. But, just before he got to it, I reached down, pulled the trigger, and unloaded a live blank. A big bang and a lot of smoke filled the classroom. My volunteer fell to the floor, grasping his abdominal area as if shot.

Then I reminded everyone that though the objective of the class was to learn care and cleaning of their M14 rifles, safety should always came first.

As you can imagine, after my class, I got run up to the old man, and I was damn near kicked out of school for that stunt. It took some doing, but I was able to justify my tactic and convince him I'd made my point and was just practicing how to grab the audience's attention—something I'd learned in that good old MCI course. I got a little more attention than I'd wanted, but I did get an A in the class. I damn sure had their undivided attention.

In the military, leadership principles are tested at the highest standards possible—in combat. When you and your unit go into harm's way, under fire, not only are you fighting for survival but also to destroy the enemy forces that are trying to destroy *you*. Failure is unthinkable. You have been equipped and trained to fight, and only under strong leadership will you fight with determination and confidence. If you lose, you die. Without leadership, your unit will fall apart, and all personal and unit efforts will be lost.

You see this principle demonstrated superbly in *Full Metal Jacket* when Private Cowboy is thrust into command of his unit because of the death of his squad leader. When he and his squad are pinned down behind a wall, lost in a combat zone, he has no idea what to do because he hasn't learned his job, he lacks knowledge (he can't even read a map), and he certainly isn't ready to lead a squad in combat.

Just being in a position of leadership didn't instantly make him a leader. *You have to be prepared in knowledge and character.*

In Cowboy's case, he'd never held a position of leadership in peacetime, let alone in combat. Sometimes, because of circumstances, promotions do come as a surprise. When this happens, it's usually not the result of a best-case scenario.

I don't have a problem with *potential* leaders taking charge *when it's necessary*—even when, under normal circumstances, they need more experience, training, and knowledge. I do, however, have a problem with *pushing* people into leadership too soon, before they're ready. Most leaders instinctively know when they've fully prepared themselves and are ready to take the reins and drive the wagon. And if they haven't already recognized it, a good commander will tell them. He'll notice when young leaders have earned the respect of others and are ready to slide over and take charge, and he'll also encourage them to be respectful of limits—reminding them that their capacity for leadership is limited by their capacity for earning others' respect, and earning respect can take time and experience.

That also means this: Not only do you evolve into leadership, but if you want to expand your leadership potential, you can't just stop where you are—you have to keep expanding your own knowledge and abilities. This constant striving for self-improvement, important for any leader, might seem daunting, but if you're smart, you'll recognize that the way to eat a huge plate of grits is one bite at a time.

Sometimes people look at their leader, and think, "Boy, I wish I were like him. But I could never do that. He's a natural-born leader. Everybody admires and respects him so much."

USMC—NO FINER MANAGEMENT SCHOOL IN THE WORLD

I thoroughly enjoy watching episodes of *Undercover Boss*. It's always amazing to me to watch CEOs get fired from their own companies because they don't know how to run a grill in the kitchen, handle a cash register, or satisfy customers who call in with questions about the product their own company sells.

The problem with some of these leaders is that they didn't ever do the jobs of the individuals they employ. How can a leader really lead if he or she doesn't understand what the people below them do on a day-to-day basis?

In contrast, the Sergeant Major of the Marine Corps—the enlisted CEO, if you will, has excellent knowledge, and in some cases, absolute mastery, of the jobs performed by those in his command. If you ask, me, there's no better model for leadership training than the United States Marine Corps.

Here's how it works:

Every enlistee starts out in the Marine Corps as a recruit and, if he or she makes it through boot camp, becomes a Private upon graduating.

Once he outgrows the rank of Private by obtaining knowledge and experience, he is recommended for Private First Class (PFC) by a superior.

After six months in grade as PFC, he is eligible for promotion to Lance Corporal.

However, not until his mentors and trainers feel he is trained, qualified, and ready will the PFC be advanced to the rank of Lance Corporal.

Little by little, as Marines attain rank, they acquire more responsibility and are responsible for more troops.

First, a Lance Corporal is put in charge of three to four troops of lower grade. Then as a Corporal, he or she is made responsible for twelve to fifteen junior troops. As a Sergeant, he directs forty to fifty troops. Staff Sergeants lead seventy to seventy-five, including the Sergeant. The company gunny commands as many as three hundred troops. And so it goes, up the ranks.

And it works this way all the way to the top pay grade of Sergeant Major of the Marine Corps—who got his start as a recruit and is responsible for every enlisted person in the Corps.

I'm sure you get the idea here. The Marine Corps hires from within. And it's designed this way so that along with responsibility come leadership skills and management capabilities.

At the end of the day, everyone in leadership has walked in the shoes of those they command. Their position of leadership has come after a gradual process of evolution. They've all been there, done that. Which, if you ask me, is as it should be.

When the troops think that way, they're not considering the time it took that leader to evolve and achieve the rank or station in life he now occupies. He earned the right to lead; it wasn't just handed to him. I'll say it again: leadership requires knowledge, and knowledge is something all of us can acquire if we apply ourselves. He might have started earlier than you did, he might have been squared away faster than you were, but there's no reason you can't evolve into a leader as well.

Sure, there are people who have some natural gifts and abilities. The captain of the high school football team is likely a natural athlete. But that doesn't mean someone else can't aspire to the position. It might take more effort, determination, time, and guts for someone who isn't so naturally inclined, but I maintain that with hard work and desire, most folks can attain what they set their minds to.

The difficulties of military leadership have been characterized by one of the greatest leaders of all time, General George C. Marshall, World War II Army chief of staff and the man who lent his name to the Marshall Plan that saved Europe from economic collapse after the war.

General Marshall said: "You have to lead men in war by bringing them along to endure and display qualities of fortitude that are beyond the average man's thought of what he should be expected to do. You have to inspire them when they are hungry and exhausted and desperately uncomfortable and in great danger; and only a man of positive characteristics of leadership, with the physical stamina that goes with it, can function under those conditions."

It's no surprise that individuals who emerge as strong leaders in military affairs can go on to excel in civilian life. Senior Staff NCOs who retire after twenty or thirty years' service are snapped up by civilian firms who want quality leaders. But never forget, it's the Corporals and Sergeants who have always been referred to as the "backbone of the Marine Corps." And for good reason.

Though I have admitted that I can't teach you to become a leader, there is a place I can send you that will make an immediate, huge difference in your progress.

Writer Julia Dye's book *Backbone: History, Traditions, and Leadership Lessons of Marine Corps NCOs* is a leadership book unlike any other. It includes great, readable prose, stories, and observations on outstanding leaders. It details the exact challenges they faced and the qualities that made them successful. I am so taken by this book after reading it several times that I consider this to be *the* textbook on military leadership. You cannot turn these pages without giving your leadership potential a gigantic boost.

Julia and her husband Dale Dye, a retired Marine captain, are well known for the technical advice they provide to film and television productions on military operations. Julia's skill as a writer makes this book a classic, in my opinion. I like her showing how Marine NCOs evolve into leaders over time, and how their leadership decisions and actions became game changers in both war and peace. Julia takes you to the actual boots-on-the-ground situations where NCOs stand tall in the face of danger and difficulty and emerge with troops ready to follow them to the ends of the earth.

If you're interested in the subject of leadership and don't check out this book, your coconut isn't screwed on right. Go get *Backbone*.

I'd make that an order if I could! Whether you're in the military or a civilian, you'll benefit from this book.

In trying to be Gunny-loud and Gunny-clear with thoughts on leadership, I don't want to miss pointing out that leadership ambitions might not be right for everyone. Perhaps giving your daily 120 percent in your current job, in which you feel comfortable and competent, brings you self-worth, happiness, respect, and fulfillment. If so, that's Gunny Approved™ from every standpoint. The call to step out front and lead the way isn't a fit for everyone. The truth is, some people just work and perform better when following orders instead of giving them. And that's a good thing because we always need troops with various abilities and motivations.

What matters is that you do the best you can in whatever position you are in, or aspire to.

Semper Fi!

WISDOM FROM THE GUNNY

"Management starts at home. Mom and Dad are our first and most effective role models."

—R. Lee Ermey

GUNNY'S RULES FOR LEADERS

★ LEADERS MAKE THEMSELVES HEARD

"Dear Senator...Dear Congressman...Dear Mr. President..."

Let's say you've endured just about as much as you can take over an important issue affecting your life, and you aim to start doing something about it.

The Gunny's all for that! Go ahead, get it off your chest: tell your elected leaders—the big shots pulling the strings—exactly how you feel.

A good place to start your mission is by writing a letter to your congressman in the House of Representatives and to both senators who represent your state. That's three letters you'll need. I strongly recommend that you compose your own; don't just attach your name to the form letters you see various groups urging you to sign. If you want to lend your name to a certain cause in this way, go ahead, but be aware that this particular action will not carry the weight of a personal letter. Those form letters are sent to Washington and to state government offices by the ton. They might be counted (or weighed), but they won't be read by Mr. Big or people on his staff.

Instead, make a little effort and write a personal, carefully composed letter explaining your concerns and your position on the issue. No profanity, please. You should not need cusswords to drive home the points you are trying to make as a concerned citizen—and as a voter! If you have a grand idea to help solve the problem, by all means share it; it's long past time that our leaders started tapping the commonsense solutions of people out in the workaday world.

When you write to your elected officials, make your letters as thoughtful and well written as you can make them. You want your thoughts to be clear, your concerns to be distinctly heard, your tone to be reasonable. You are a hard-working, tax-paying American citizen writing to his duly elected representative—so you should write in a matter of mutual respect, even if you think the congressman is a jackass!

And also consider writing to your state and local representatives. Politicians always say that all politics is local. Make them earn your vote by listening to you, the voter. In a free country, we're supposed to be the leaders of our communities. We're the ultimate guardians of our Republic and our Constitution. The politicians are supposed to be following *our* orders, representing the people, not their party. They're supposed to serve us, not ride roughshod over us. So let them know what you think. Stand up and be counted.

★ LEADERS EARN THEIR STRIPES

My experiences with Marine NCOs have shown me time and time again that they are outstanding leaders who have earned their stripes.

Not tolerated in their ranks is the "he doesn't like me" card used by shit-birds to blame their superiors for their screw-ups and lack of promotion. Marine NCOs and officers do not recognize the "he doesn't like me" card. Play it, and you'll be locking heels for a good ass-chewing. Trust me, if your superior doesn't like you, there is usually a damned good reason.

I have never worked with a Marine Corps officer I couldn't get along with. In fact, I have the highest admiration and respect possible for Marine officers. Most of them are college graduates, though officer ranks are open to high school graduates who qualify. Regardless, Marine officers are all trained at the Marine Corps Officers Candidate School at Quantico, Virginia. The training is as tough as anything you can imagine. Marine officers are professional, they're gentlemen or ladies, and I've never known one who ever let me down.

★ LEADERSHIP IS NOT LIMITED BY RANK

The Gunny has been fortunate in meeting and spending time with many of the last ten Commandants and Sergeants Major of the Marine Corps. My visits to the Pentagon to connect with such dignitaries for our *Mail Call* television series and other activities have been highlights of my career. Standing among such leaders is an inspirational experience, for sure, but I feel much of the same level of pride when I watch Corporals, Sergeants, and Staff NCOs leading squads, platoons, and companies. Leadership counts in every rank of the Corps.

★ REMEMBER—LEADERS AREN'T BORN, THEY EVOLVE

In case you're wondering if you fit the mold for leadership potential, relax. There is no mold!

Nobody can wave a magic wand and suddenly make you a leader. You evolve into leadership positions, gaining responsibility a little at a time while working with people in your unit or on your staff.

But if you want to be a leader, you can start by reading, learning, and striving to get better, to be the best at every aspect of your job so that you are naturally looked upon to lead and instruct others. You need to know what to do, you need to do it, and you need to be a person that others can trust and rely on. Do that, and you just might evolve into the leader you want to be.

LEADERSHIP
QUOTES WORTH REPEATING

"I tell you as officers, that you neither eat, nor drink, nor smoke, nor sit down, nor lean against a tree, until you have personally seen that your men have first had a chance to do those things. If you do this for them, they will follow you to the ends of the earth. And if you do not, I will bust you in front of your regiments."

—Field Marshal William Joseph Slim

"Authority does not make you a leader. It gives you the opportunity to be one."

—Anonymous

"I do not fear an army of lions, if they are led by a lamb. I do fear an army of sheep, if they are led by a lion."

—Alexander the Great

"The leader must know, must know that he knows, and must be able to make it abundantly clear to those around him that he knows."

—Clarence R. Randall

"I cannot give you the formula for success, but I can give you the formula for failure, which is: Try to please everybody."

—Herbert Swope

"Character is the direct result of mental attitude. I believe that character is higher than intellect. I believe that leadership is in sacrifice, in self-denial, in humility, and in the perfectly disciplined will. This is the distinction between great and little men."

—Vince Lombardi

"No man will make a great leader who wants to do it all himself, or to get all the credit for doing it."

—Andrew Carnegie

"What lies behind us and what lies before us are tiny matters compared to what lies within us."

—Oliver Wendell Holmes

"If your actions inspire others to dream more, learn more, do more and become more, you are a leader."

—John Quincy Adams

"A leader is a dealer in hope."

—Napoleon Bonaparte

"I still need Marines who can shoot and salute. But I need Marines who can fix jet engines and man sophisticated radar sets, as well."

—General Robert E. Cushman Jr., USMC

"Before you are a leader, success is all about growing yourself. When you become a leader, success is all about growing others."

—Jack Welch

"There is a great deal of talk about loyalty from the bottom to the top. Loyalty from the top down is even more necessary and much less prevalent."

—General George S. Patton Jr.

"My own definition of leadership is this: The capacity and the will to rally men and women to a common

purpose and the character which inspires confidence."

—Commander Bernard Law Montgomery

"Leadership is unlocking people's potential to become better."

—Bill Bradley

"True leaders are not those who strive to be first, but those who are first to strive and give their all for the success of the team. True leaders are first to see the need, envision the plan, and empower the team for action. By the strength of the leader's commitment, the power of the team is unleashed."

—Unknown

CHAPTER

LOOK OUT, WORLD!

THE GUNNY IS PISSED

It's rant time, and to hell with political correctness. The Gunny will spare no sacred cows as he calls your attention to cleaning up the mess we're in and getting life squared away.

MY DAY IN COURT

It is three o'clock in the morning, and I am pissed off! So pissed off, as a matter of fact, that I can't sleep.

My tossing and turning has now upset Mrs. Gunny to the point that she orders me out of the bedroom. I have been exiled to my War Room (a "man cave" in the civilian world) until such time as I can gain control of my unstable state of mind. And be a good boy!

Thinking she might be a bit more understanding and possibly even sympathetic, I tried to explain my predicament. She answered with a tone of voice and facial expression bordering on insubordination, then sarcastically suggested I write my problems on a list she might read while having her coffee after letting out the dogs in the morning. But right now, she wanted me to get the hell out and let her sleep. "Sympathy," she curtly barked as I made my way toward the door, "could be found in the dictionary somewhere between shit and syphilis."

Lord only knows who she's been hanging out with to pick up that sharp tongue.

So . . . I'm in my War Room now. This is my domain. Here, I rule! Excuse me, world. Can I be in charge for a while? Thank you very much.

I think I'll fire up a nice stinky cigar, maybe even let off a little gas.

That's better. There's a little itch down around my pubic area. Come on, Erm, give it a good scratch. I might even pick at this old scab on my hand if I feel like it. After all, I call the shots here in my War Room.

The dilemma that put me here, totally pissed off, actually began a few months back. An officer of the law pulled me over and wrote me up for not wearing my seat belt while I was driving my Jeep Wrangler. Had I been in my truck or car, I would have been buckled up. The seat belt idea, as I understand it, is to keep you securely fastened to your seat in the event of an accident. If the vehicle were to roll over, the belt would keep you from being hurled around inside, bashing your skull, breaking bones, and receiving other serious injuries. But if you are in a vehicle that has no top, your only hope is to be thrown clear when it rolls. My Wrangler had no top and no roll bar. No top, no roll bar . . . you're strapped into your seatbelt . . . you roll . . . you die! It's real simple.

The officer was not receptive to my commonsense logic. She gave me a ticket anyway.

So yesterday found me lined up with your run-of-the-mill accused speeders, thieves, wife-beaters, swindlers, and other outcasts at the Lancaster County courthouse. Of course, a lot of people there recognized me since I'm on TV. Hell, the guy sitting next to me in the courtroom asked me to autograph his traffic citation.

While we waited, I needed to use the restroom—which is where my state of mind began its months-long escalation into the "pissed off" zone.

As soon as I entered the crapper stall, the automatic toilet flushed. As I sat taking care of business, the damned thing flushed five more times, spitting cold water up onto my butt, and then once more before I could clear the stall. This waste tightened my jaws.

Due to a critical lack of rain this year, water restrictions were imposed on the good citizens of the high desert area where I live. If caught washing your car, watering your lawn, or otherwise wasting water, you'd be imposed a heavy fine. So, my car was dirty and my lawn was brown and dead from lack of water, but this stupid automatic crapper had needlessly flushed seven times.

Are we Americans so damn helpless and lazy we can't flush a toilet?

Sitting in the courtroom with a hundred other people, waiting for the judge to arrive, I was mulling over the idea of bringing the toilet situation to the judge's attention. No, I decided. I would stick with my game plan of pointing out to the judge that using the seat belt on my Wrangler would be like using a seat belt on a motorcycle. Judges are smart people. Surely he would see the logic. All charges would be dropped. Then I would mention the toilets flushing unnecessarily. And we'd be on our way to the seat belt laws being revised and automatic toilets being fixed or returned to stick shift mode. Made sense to me.

> **Are we Americans so damned helpless and lazy we can't flush a toilet?**

The Gunny was ready to take the stand.

The judge entered the courtroom an hour late. "All rise! Court is in session, the honorable Judge Muckity Muck presiding. Be seated."

The judge spoke into a microphone. "Folks, here's how it works in my courtroom. When your name is called, you will step forward. Charges will be read. I will ask how you plead. You will answer 'guilty' or 'not guilty.' Nothing more. Nothing less. No song-and-dance explanations. No excuses."

The judge recognized me from TV, but that didn't stop him from fining me $350.

We never did address the water problem in the head. God, I hate the idiot who invented that wasteful autothrone.

I went home, washed my truck, watered my dead lawn, and put a "For Sale" sign on the Wrangler.

And that is why, months later, I'm sitting in my War Room at zero dark three thirty in the morning, totally pissed off, and putting it down on paper for you, Mrs. Gunny, and anybody else who will bother to listen.

By the way, I am not whining. I'm simply pointing out stupid crap that needs fixing.

Matter of fact, as long as I'm in the mood, I'll keep this list going and get some other issues off my chest.

Stay with me.

AUTOMATIC OVERKILL: WE'VE HAD ENOUGH!

I recently received a very disturbing phone call from my youngest daughter, who is going to school in San Diego. "Dad, some lady ran into my car while I was sitting at a stoplight. It's totaled. I need a new one right away so I can get to school and work."

Being the wonderful father that I am, I started shopping. I wanted something basic—simple transportation. Evonne didn't need GPS; I'd taught her how to read a map. She didn't need power windows and power door locks that lock the doors even if you don't want them locked, or power seats and seat heaters. Come on. We live in southern California. What the hell do we need seat heaters for? Or power mirrors, especially on the driver's side?

The problem is that all this power stuff starts breaking after you've had the car a few years, and the car begins spending more time in the shop than it does on the road. And the more it's in the shop, the more opportunities for you to spend an arm and a leg at the hands of rip-off-artist mechanics.

Such as the time I drove from California to visit my relations in Kansas, and the driver's side window quit working in Colorado, stuck in the open position. It was winter. I froze my butt off for one hundred miles before I gave in and pulled into some small-town rip-off joint to get it fixed. My truck is only three years old, but it wasn't long ago that the driver's side power mirror quit working, and now it will not adjust manually. Good thing I'm the only one who drives it.

Some of these seemingly convenient electronic luxuries could actually cause your death. If you are unconscious after a crash, and the vehicle is on fire, locked doors can keep rescuers from pulling you to safety. If you happen to slide into a river, water would render the car's battery useless. Without power, the windows would not go down and the door locks would not function. No escape! What a great way to die—sitting there, waiting for your car to fill up with water so you can drown!

Why have we allowed Detroit to do this to us?

GRATUITIES

Gratuities (or tips) are given as a form of reward, usually to the underpaid folks employed in the service industry: valets, barbers, taxi drivers, waiters, and bartenders. My concern is with the most *vulnerable* of them, the waiter and waitress. I have always been a generous tipper. I have plenty, and I don't mind sharing it.

In my view, if you receive good service, a good tip is in order.

However, somewhere along the way, some self-appointed etiquette nerd decided that a 15-percent tip is appropriate no matter what, and now, in most places, it just shows up, prefigured into my tab! For one thing, I know how to calculate 15 percent, thank you very much. For another, I'll be the judge of the amount of tip I feel is proper.

The bigger problem is, this system leaves things open for unscrupulous restaurant and hotel owners and managers to abuse the time-honored tradition of tipping. In this day and age, the tip has been reduced to little more than a bargaining chip for management and an excuse to underpay their kitchen help and servers.

I'm co-owner of a pub myself, and I guarantee we will never take tipping out of our customers' hands.

If you pay by credit card, the tip meant for your minimum-wage waiter or waitress can easily end up in the hands of a greedy manager. In some cases, management takes it upon themselves to divide up your tip among the kitchen help. In my view, management has no right to automatically receive the tip money meant for the waiter or waitress and shared as he or she sees fit with the cook, the dishwasher, and the busboy. If you want to tip the kitchen crew or the cook or anyone else, it should be up to you, not management.

To help right this wrong, do what I do: always give your reward to the waiter or waitress in cash. Never add your gratutity to the tab.

PETA'S PET

Hey, did you hear that PETA, People for the Ethical Treatment of Animals, has demanded that Mercedes Benz stop putting luxury seats into their cars? And now Mercedes has agreed to start making $80,000 cars with cloth seats. Well isn't that sweet! Mr. and Mrs. Butter Cow won't have to worry about becoming an upgrade in an E350. Maybe even someday their little calf can go to college. Bullshit. Now what do these PETA people think we raise cows for? Pets? Companionship?

They're raised for milk, meat, and leather, damn it. When its time is up, a cow is rendered from snout to tail—nothing goes to waste. Even its hoofs could end up on your dessert plate. We butcher our cattle for food, then use what we can from the carcass. What are we supposed to do with the hide of a dead cow? Throw it away? Nothing goes to waste, PETA!

I'd like to see those so-called animal lovers get by for just one day trying not to eat, wear, or put their pretty little bottoms on something that doesn't come from an animal. It can't be done! But go ahead, PETA, give it a try. But don't call this old Marine for help, because I'll be out deer hunting.

WHEN TEACHERS GET FAILING GRADES

If you have children, the only way they'll have a fair shot at a decent life is through a good education. Can your kids read? Have you given up on public schools and the union-protected losers who claim to be educators?

How many times have you heard teachers moaning about overcrowded classrooms (making excuses) and children who come to school without receiving proper discipline at home (more excuses).

Back in the day before unions, teachers could be fired for being lazy and nonproductive. Dismissal was a sure thing if they came to work and it turned out that they were not able to teach. (Oh, for the good old days!)

Our public school systems went to hell when the government started calling the shots and got in bed with unions.

When a student fails to learn, it's because the teacher failed to teach! Perhaps the student's particular problem is beyond the scope of the teacher's experience and training—in which case, the obvious answer is for the school to hire an extra tutor (not another bureaucrat; we all know how the education bureaucracy is one of the fattest around). But what we usually get from the school system is endless whining and complaining and demands for more and more money without giving parents better results.

You want better schools? Here's an idea: break the education bureaucracy and self-serving unions by privatizing the whole damn school system. If we taxpayer-parents are going to get value for our money, let us shop around. You know what, we'll choose the best schools, with the best teachers, at the best prices—and that means with the fewest feather-bedding fat-cat bureaucrats. And you know who will benefit most? The kids! (Not to mention the best teachers—and your taxes should go down, too.) So let's do it!

SHARKS EAT STUFF—INCLUDING DIVERS

Apparently we're supposed to believe that sharks attack people because of a case of mistaken identity, that the poor sharks think we're seals.

I recently watched a video of great white sharks trying their damndest to bust through the bars of an underwater cage and eat the terrified divers inside. You'd think images like those would be game changers for phony nature lovers. But no, these hand-wringing Nature Nannies, who won't go near the water themselves, proclaim that sharks are misunderstood, that they're really okay, and that the poor sight-impaired killers believed they'd found the mother of all seal packs.

Bullshit!

Okay, fine. So they're nearly blind. Still, I can guarantee you it's not a case of mistaken anything. Sharks have an incredible sense of smell—and I'll bet you my scuba tank that I don't smell anything like a seal.

> **Apparently we're supposed to believe that sharks attack people because of a case of mistaken identity. Bullshit!**

I enjoyed diving for many years when stationed in Okinawa and the Philippines and still have all my fingers and toes because I never let my guard down. I'm pissed when some misguided pseudo-ecologist tries to tell me I'm full of shit for thinking sharks are dangerous.

They don't bite off arms and legs by accident. When you swim into their domain, sometimes they swim away, and sometimes they don't swim away. It all depends on whether they're hungry.

This "let's be friends" attitude has cost the arms, legs, and lives of divers and surfers who either ignored the warnings or just don't get it: Sharks own the place!

BAMBI DOESN'T LIVE HERE ANYMORE

The tree huggers make me want to puke. They profess to love nature and know more about what's right and wrong between man and nature than anybody else. Mostly, their ranks are filled with Bambi-influenced, brainwashed bleeding hearts who wouldn't know a loon from a Canada goose if it crapped on their heads.

You can't tell a tree hugger that we need to harvest timber where a few spotted owls live, or that fisheries have a right to keep out marauding sea lions.

The word "hunting" makes tree huggers feel like calling the police. They'll never hear a word you try to tell them about the reality that whitetail deer need to be harvested, not even if you're standing in front of the smashed-in hood of their car after a run-in with a deer from an overpopulated herd. Hunters have a legitimate, state-approved right to harvest deer, putting food on their tables and keeping the herd population at numbers the environment can sustain.

When the deer herd becomes so large that the animals consume more than the terrain can sustain, the animals are forced into human habitat, searching for food. They cause accidents on roads and highways, damage property, and eventually have die-offs from starvation and disease.

Try telling that to a tree hugger. I hope you have better luck than I have.

THOSE FAST-LANE INTRUDERS

You're cruising along the turnpike and need to get into the left lane, the fast lane, to use it for the purpose it is intended—to pass other vehicles. Instead, you find yourself stuck in the left lane behind some slow-moving asshole who stays there like he owns it. The mind reels at the number of accidents caused by these left-lane slowpokes. Their stupidity causes faster vehicles to make lane changes, at speed, often in heavy traffic.

I'll give you ten to one that many left-lane crawlers don't even know the law—that the left lane is for passing. And if they don't know that law, how many other rules of the road are AWOL in their coconuts?

I'm getting even more pissed off just thinking about it.

GLOBAL WARMING: IT'S A STICKUP!

Looking for a government grant? Then you'd better agree that global warming exists and is threatening our planet.

Weather change is as inevitable as the two other things we can't do anything about— death and taxes.

The scientists, ecologists, and other researchers who are ranting about the possibility (and that's all it is, a "possibility") of global warming want one thing: funding. They want your tax dollars to support years of cushy jobs and benefits while they dick around with this theory and that theory, with many, many conferences and travel expenses thrown in. From universities to state offices, to the federal government, all the way to the UN, the researchers are thrusting one hand into our wallets while waving the finger of their other hand in our faces, warning that if we don't pay up and support their efforts, we'll lose our planet.

Bullshit! The Gunny is not convinced that any warming—if any really exists—isn't part of a natural cycle the earth has experienced since day one. The test-tube jockeys who want the government to support their work will sell us out and agree with Al Gore on global warning, or they won't get their grants.

I've lived in the high desert country of California for over thirty years. Last winter, for the first time ever, outside water pipes froze and broke. Didn't look like global warming to me. As far as I'm concerned, weather change is as inevitable as the two other things we can't do anything about—death and taxes.

I DON'T WANT TO FREEZE IN THE DARK!

Environmentalists blocking the Keystone Pipeline project and oil and natural gas exploration in Alaska and offshore sites are making us more dependent on foreign oil and keeping The Gunny pissed off.

Number one on my list of sites that would help make us self-sufficient is the Arctic National Wildlife Refuge (ANWAR), which I have visited a couple of times. ANWAR is like a freaking wasteland, not the wilderness paradise the environmentalists would like the world to believe.

I'm in agreement with most Alaskans, who dearly love their wild-life and consider their wild place a natural refuge, that we can drill there without serious consequences.

We have learned much from the mistakes of the past, and the plain fact is that we need domestic oil and gas exploration to stop the Middle Eastern oil sheik-down of our economy.

SECOND AMENDMENT RIGHTS UNDER FIRE

I am a board member for the NRA for the simple reason that I want to be in the trenches, on the front line, opposing the relentless media forces and others who seem determined to strip away our Second Amendment rights and take our guns.

Of course I'm devastated when I learn about violent tragedies like the shooting that took place at Sandy Hook. However, the hysteria caused by politicians who got whipped into a frenzy because they suddenly wanted to show they were "doing something about guns" just pisses me off.

I was at the NRA meeting directly after that incident, and guess what? We were followed by armed guards—for our protection.

The misinformation, the sheer lunacy about guns that has been dished out to the American public by self-aggrandizing politicians and their media mouthpieces is mind-boggling.

Our opposition to the moves to rewrite the Second Amendment, which is the initial step toward taking away our guns, must be as strong and relentless as the moves by those who want to attack our freedom. Our right to own guns for hunting, recreational shooting, and home protection is at stake.

It's a cliché, but it's true: Guns don't kill people. People kill people. Wake up, America! Do the background checks. I'm all for it.

To me, the threat posed by emotionally or socially unstable individuals only fortifies the logic of having self-protection, which a gun provides for the 99.99 percent of decent, law-abiding gun owners out there.

Frankly, at times I find myself wishing I had a permit for concealed carry. State laws on concealed carry vary considerably, and my home state of California makes it so difficult that I would be wasting my time.

In 2012, according to the NRA's Institute for Legislative Action, in forty-one of forty-four states with right-to-carry laws, violent crime was at a thirty-seven-year low.[*] Does the press show that? Hell no! They rant and rave about right-wing states that pass right-to-carry laws; then when the media sees right-to-carry cuts crime, they drop the subject from their radar altogether.

With all the lunacy out there, I believe it behooves everyone to have self- and home-protection. Who knows when or where we'll

---

[*] "Right to Carry 2012," NRA-ILA February 28, 2012, http://www.nraila.org/gun-laws/articles/2012/right-to-carry-2012.aspx.

encounter some ill-intentioned person with a gun or a knife or even a bomb. You can't tell what's coming. It's hard to cover all the bases, but you've got to try and figure out how to protect yourself and your loved ones as best you can.

One of the biggest problems in our country these days is home invasion. If you're a victim of an invasion and don't have a home protection system (a gun!), don't come crying to me when it's too late. When seconds count, the police are usually minutes away.

The politicians say they will protect us. Bullshit! They want our guns—and knives—while they build the Nanny State. I can't understand today's politicians, supposedly smart leaders, who can't figure out that the criminals are not going to turn in or register their guns. In the society the anti-gun coalition would create, it's the honest, law-abiding citizen who would be left defenseless.

That's where we're headed if we allow them to trample our Second Amendment rights.

IMMIGRATION AND ILLEGALS

The immigration mess and enormous population of illegals here in California is a huge daily headache for taxpayers. Our tax bills continue to soar under a government that provides healthcare, education, welfare, and a full plate of other benefits to people who are in this country illegally. Now California is even issuing driver's licenses to illegal immigrants. The problem is so blatant here in California that I have strongly considered moving out. But I've been here so long that the escape hatch seems to be closing, locking me in.

I love and respect our hardworking brothers and sisters from the south who have gone the extra mile and respected this country enough to immigrate legally into the United States. I have traveled to nearly half the countries in the world. But not once have I entered another country without first obtaining the blessings of that country's government in the form of a visa.

With that being said, I can't find it in my heart to lay full blame on those who seek a better life for themselves. If I were struggling to survive in Mexico and looking across the border at all the benefits and opportunities available in the United States, I would probably be trying as hard as I could to make the United States my new home as well.

I can't say I blame them, especially when it's almost as if our government were setting a welcome table for them, adding more and more to the feast, while at the same time telling the American people it is doing everything it can to keep illegal immigrants out. The fact is, our elected leaders haven't the foggiest idea who is coming across our borders—and they don't seem to care!

> **All I can expect right now is to remain pissed!**

It seems to me that the message from some politicians is, "I don't care how you get here, just as long as you vote for me once you're here. Have some food stamps."

All I can expect right now is to remain pissed!

THE CANCER THAT WELFARE HAS BECOME

The Welfare State that we have permitted and actually nurtured here in America is a cancer that will destroy our society if allowed to go unchecked.

We now have generations of Americans who have never held jobs, never even bothered looking for a job, because they are content to live off Uncle Sam—courtesy of you and me!

The last time I checked, "lazy" is a condition, not a disability. I'm all for helping the good, honest people in our country who, through no fault of their own, find themselves in need.

I will help my neighbor, but I refuse to support my neighbor if he's not willing to at least try to support himself. It's about time that more people in this country started doing their jobs—starting with our elected officials but including everyone else, from teachers to parents, from the teen who could get off his ass and into the service to the college graduate who might need to flip burgers until he finds that perfect job. Get out there and get to work!

CHAPTER

PARTING SHOTS

THE GUNNY'S FAVORITE THINGS

I don't just rant. Sometimes I issue a hearty thumbs-up on a matter, product, or organization I believe in. Here are few I'm passionate enough about to consider Gunny Approved™!

RIDE ON, GUNNY! RIDE ON!

It started with an ancient motorbike called a "Cushman Eagle" before I went into the Marines as a teenager. The pull of the open road, rolling the power on, the sound of the engine growling and the rush of air past my head. The sensations were irresistible.

They still are. My teenage years are a distant memory, but I still look forward to enjoying those same sensations every chance I get, especially when I'm home after being on the road, crammed into airplanes, hotels, and endless meetings. The roads in the high desert where I live beckon, and when I accelerate the power on one of today's bikes, I feel as if I'm launching a small personal adventure, using my free time, enjoying the road for two or three hours at a time.

I aim to haul ass on a bike into geezerhood and beyond. My plan is to semi-retire when I'm ninety-two, but I'll ride till I die.

One reason I'm so confident is that I'm a safe rider; I follow the rules and laws, and I always use common sense. Sometimes when the road is clear and conditions are squared away, I may go a little fast. But I'm never showing off, and I never put myself or others in danger. From experience, I know how to read the road ahead for trouble spots—loose gravel, tight turns, traffic slowing, or cars backing up.

I ride a Victory Motorcycle custom-painted in Marine Corps colors.

I won't ride without my leather jacket and a helmet. Hell, as far as I'm concerned, the leathers are just as important as the helmet.

I prefer wearing sunglasses rather than a helmet shield. But, for going out on the open road, I do like to have a windscreen on my bike. You young pups go ahead and enjoy the 70 mph wind and tasty bugs. These days I prefer my bugs grilled, with a little seasoning, thank you very much. Not being young anymore, I prefer comfort.

I ride a Victory Motorcycle custom-painted in Marine Corps colors. I've been the Victory spokesperson for a few years now, and I can tell you these made-in-the-USA machines have never let me down. You can check them out online at www.victorymotorcycles.com, and you can see The Gunny doing his thing with Victory Motorcycles on Victory's YouTube channel.

REGISTERING TO VOTE: GET IT DONE!

The Gunny has no respect for people who do not register to vote and exercise the basic citizenship right that so many have sacrificed their time and lives to protect. I have such strong feelings about the subject that I made a video about it for the NRA's Freedom Action Foundation. It's a pretty darn good video, too, if I must say so myself. Check it out on YouTube by searching the title, "Peace and Quiet."

While you're at your computer, search for the U.S. Election Assistance Commission, and check out their resources for voters, including voter guides, registration information, voting accessibility, and information for military and overseas voters.

To be eligible to vote, you must be a U.S. citizen. In most states, you must be eighteen years old to vote, but some states do allow seventeen-year-olds to vote in primary elections. Individual states also have their own residency requirements to vote. For additional information about state-specific requirements and voter eligibility, contact your state election office.

Get it done! And that's an order, damn it!

THE TALLEST MARINES

They're thirty-two feet high, looming eighty feet above you, and when you raise your head to focus your eyes on the six Marines hoisting the flag on Iwo Jima at the Marine Corps War Memorial in Washington, you'll feel an irresistible surge of pride. The plaque on the statue says it is in honor of all Marines who have given their lives since November 1775, when the Corps was founded. I feel that the flag-raising Marines represent the guts and determination of every Marine who has ever pulled on a pair of combat boots and served our country—bless 'em all, the long, the short, and the tall.

When my dear friend Jack Lucas was buried in his hometown of Hattiesburg, Mississippi, my thoughts were dominated by images of those Marines at Mount Suribachi on Iwo Jima. I was unable to attend Jack's funeral, but I know that he had a Marine coffin and full military honors befitting a Medal of Honor recipient. As far as I'm concerned, we should have a bronze statue of Jack Lucas.

Jack was awarded the Medal of Honor by President Harry S. Truman in October of 1945 for his courage on Iwo Jima the previous February. Jack was one of nine Medal of Honor recipients who survived the Battle of Iwo Jima. The other thirteen Medal of Honor awards for exceptional courage on Iwo—the most ever for any single U.S. battle—were made posthumously, to heroes who did not make it home.

I crossed paths frequently with Jack at military ceremonies over the years, and I was proud of his friendship. On February 20, 1945, Jack and four other Marines were in a face-to-face firefight with enemy soldiers defending the two airfields on Iwo Jima that were the invasion's main objective. Firing point-blank at the enemy until his M1 jammed, Jack spotted two grenades that landed in the foxhole next to him and his fellow Marines. Jack threw himself over the first grenade and pulled the second one under his body. The first grenade exploded, severely wounding him and leaving him unable to move. Jack told me the next five minutes were the longest of his life as he waited for the second grenade to go off, which miraculously turned out to be a dud.

Private Jack Lucas was only seventeen years old at the time. Tough and muscular, even as a boy, he had lied about his age to enter the Marines at the age of fourteen. In 1945, not yet having seen combat, he left his unit in Hawaii and stowed away on a troopship to join the action on Iwo.

Skillful corpsmen saved Jack's life. Though his wounds were a serious handicap, with time and surgery he went on to live a total of eighty-four happy, productive years.

Jack went back to Iwo in 2005, and I was with him. The occasion was to commemorate the sixtieth anniversary of the battle. I was there with my *Mail Call* crew to film what ultimately would become two show segments meant to tell the world about the almost-insurmountable obstacles our Marines faced on Iwo.

It was an honor to have Jack on-camera in my shows, but he had his own special way to tell the folks here at home about Iwo: he wrote a book about it.

The book is called *Indestructible*, by Jack H. Lucas, with D. K. Drum, published by Da Capo Press in 2006. It has a wonderful fore-word by another hero, Senator Bob Dole, who was badly wounded in the fighting in Italy as a soldier in World War II. The book is a great read.

I was really struck by the way the cover of *Indestructible* takes us to the heart of this battle, which is now a landmark event in military history. In the cover photograph taken from National Archives film footage, Marines are struggling up the black-lava sand dunes on the beaches at Iwo. Unlike most views of the lava dunes, this one reveals the deadly slopes that were *beyond* the dunes, where Japanese soldiers committed to fighting to their deaths were raining sheets of bullets, artillery shells, and mortars onto the beaches. Entrenched in bunkers, machine-gun nests, and foxholes—many of them connected by eighteen-plus miles of tunnels—the twenty-two thousand Japanese soldiers sworn to defend the island and its airfields poured withering fire at the invading Marines from positions on Mount Suribachi, the bluffs beyond the beaches, and the perimeters of the airfield. Only about two hundred Japanese, some of them conscripted Korean laborers, survived the thirty-six-day battle. Our Marines lost 6,800 dead and suffered twenty-two thousand wounded.

Like Jack Lucas, I did my best with my two *Mail Call* shows to bring the Iwo Jima experience home to the American people. *Mail Call* can still be viewed on the History Channel's Military Channel, and DVD copies of many segments are available at my Gunny PX, www.rleeermey.com. The two Iwo Jima specials are in *The Best of Mail Call*, number six. The Battle of Iwo Jima was special, and Joe Rosenthal's photograph is probably the single most viewed photograph in America. That photograph inspired the statue, the Iwo Jima War Memorial, which continues to inspire—and I trust will inspire countless generations of Americans to come.

And in case you haven't gotten the word, when you're in the D.C. area, you do not want to miss the National Marine Corps Museum located just outside Quantico, Virginia. As a museum of military history and heritage, it is second to none. Check it out at www. usmcmuseum.org.

VETERANS SERVICES ORGANIZATIONS: THE COMPLETE LIST

The U.S. Department of Veterans Affairs offers a complete directory of veterans services organizations. You can download a PDF of the directory at www.va.gov/vso/. You'll find all the info you need to make contact with various organizations.

"CARRYING ON" WITH TRU-SPEC

If you happen to come across a gray-haired gentleman making his way through the airport with an effective-looking, military-style backpack instead of the usual carry-on rigs, you just might be crossing paths with mc on onc of my missions.

The backpack will be Tru-Spec's Signature Gunny Line "Tour of Duty" backpack, which I helped them design. The company—which, by the way, does its own manufacturing—also produces my Lightweight Tactical Trousers (boot-cut, thank you very much), my Tactical Shirt, my Tactical Vest, and my Eight-Point Cover. The shirt and trousers are so comfortable I wear them all the time.

I became Tru-Spec's spokesperson after coming to them because I was so impressed with their reputation for quality. We got together on my ideas, and now I'm behind the finished products 100 percent.

The Tour of Duty pack will serve you equally well whether you're using it as an airplane carry-on or packing it out in the bush, hunting, hiking, or fishing. When I'm traveling, with careful packing I can carry three days' supplies of everything I need.

Check out Tru-Spec products at their web site, www.truspec.com. You can see their videos there or by going to YouTube and searching for titles starting with "Gunny Tru-Spec Videos."

SOG SPECIALTY KNIVES & TOOLS: THE CUTTING EDGE

When I first became associated with SOG Specialty Knives & Tools, the company's founder, Spencer Frazer, cut me loose to design and help develop the Gunny Fixed Blade and Gunny Folding Knife. They make knives for every purpose, from everyday pocketknives to machetes, multi-tools, flashlights, and survival blades that can bring you back alive from a tight spot out in the wild.

I once read about a couple of hikers who died after getting lost in the woods. They were unable to build fires and shelter. They did not have food or the proper clothing to withstand the cold and wet of an overnight storm. Their cell phones were useless with run-down batteries. And they did not have a knife or flashlight. They had only gone out for a simple afternoon hike, not an overnight survival experience, and died of exposure.

For me—and I'm betting for you as well—a simple afternoon hike requires some kind of fanny pack or backpack, with flashlight, matches, and an all-important knife. In some cases, I might even be carrying two knives, a folder and a fixed blade in a sheath on my belt. I doubt that I will lose my way and have to spend the night in the woods, but I guarantee that if that's the case, I will be walking out of there the next morning.

There in the woods, my knife will give me fuzz sticks and small slices of tiny kindling I can use to create a small fire, one that will grow larger and larger as I add bigger branches and logs. With my knife, I'll cut the limbs and branches I need to make a shelter. Even if it's just a crude lean-to, it will be good for some protection from the elements. My knife will save my life.

Knives are tools that will do just about anything your mission requires, from cutting fishing bait to dressing out an elk. They have fascinated me since my grandfather gave me my first pocketknife when I was a kid. (I still have that knife, by the way.)

Here's the way I describe my love affair with knives on the SOG website:

> It is said that the dawn of human intelligence and civilization can be traced to the emergence of tools—flint knives and spear heads—during prehistoric times.
>
> And ever since, there has been a unique bond and relationship between humanity and the knives and tools we use. These instruments mean much more to us than the

functions they provide. They symbolize independence, ingenuity, self-sufficiency, strength and confidence. With them, we feel prepared for any situation and in control of our environment and destiny.

I often think back to when my grandfather gave me my first knife, a pocket-knife. It meant more to me than just a nifty, sharp-edged tool. It meant that he felt I was ready for responsibility, that it was time to begin to leave childhood behind. It was time to become accountable, productive. That's a rite of passage that I am sure most of you can relate to and an experience we need to keep alive for young people today.

Knives and tools can be an important vehicle for helping teach children about responsibility, accountability, confidence and character. We need to help foster a relationship for them with knives and tools—as we had done for us—so that they, too, can come to understand that it is within their power to conquer any situation and provide for themselves.

I highly recommend a visit to the SOG website, www.SOGknives. com, and that you take a look at the videos I've made for SOG. They're on YouTube, where you can search for "Gunny Ermey Does SOG."

THE BOOK ANTI-HUNTERS REALLY HATE

Here's a book so good and useful that I've just got to pass along the word. It's called *The Politically Incorrect Guide to Hunting*, by Frank Miniter. There's nothing that flaky left-wingers hate more than hunting, and here's a book that blows the anti-hunters' viewpoints all to hell. Miniter's book shreds every anti-hunting argument to pieces. Here are a couple of samples straight from the jacket copy:

Did you know?

- How hunters are wildlife's best defenders—far more effective than big-budget 'green' groups.
- How deer cause more human deaths each year than sharks, cougars, bears, and alligators combined.
- Why hunting is statistically safer for kids than football, bicycling, and tennis.

If you're a hunter, you've got to have this book to help you tell the next anti-hunter you meet to shove it! It's available at your favorite bookstore or online.

TRUE STORY: HOW ONE FAMILY COPES WITH DEPLOYMENT

Don't miss this book: *Video Games and Machine Guns: A Wyoming Marine in Afghanistan*, by Thomas K. O'Neal. (Available from the author at www.videogamesandmachineguns.com.)

Tom handed me a signed copy of his book at a SHOT Show. He and his wife were in the Army, and the Marine in the book is their son. The book gives you some idea of the sufferings and the sacrifices of the sons and daughters who have stepped up to the plate and are currently over there. It puts you right in their shoes, fighting the Taliban in the notorious Helmand Province. It shows how this particular family endured the fighting, how they communicated, the organizations they belonged to, and how they stick together with other families in similar situations and with the same concerns.

SHOOTING FOR FUN: JOIN GUNNY ON THE RANGE

Each year, I look forward to the days when my rifle team will be on the firing line in the Creedmoor competitive matches throughout the United States, culminating in the National Rifle Championships at Camp Perry, Ohio, in late July and early August.

Our team includes Dennis DeMille, Donny Trump (Donald Trump's son), Bob Schanen, and Carl Bernosky. We usually shoot in about ten matches every year, depending on the time I can get away. We win our share and have even set a lot of new records over the years—more than I can list here. Dennis DeMille is one such record holder. He can read the wind, he can coach, he's a hell of a guy, and—you guessed it—he's a retired Marine. He stands up there like a freaking rock. I call him "The Machine" for the way he wins national championships and sets national records.

If you like to shoot, I strongly urge you to check into both rifle and pistol competitive shooting opportunities with the NRA (NRA.org) and the National Sport Shooting Foundation (NSSF.org). The atmosphere of camaraderie and competition makes organized match shooting a recreational opportunity that can be enjoyed by individuals and families, young and old, male and female. You don't have to be afraid of being a "newbie." The experienced shooters will take you under their wings and walk you through it all. They love to help. There, you'll find coaching on safety, techniques, and gear—even a lot of tips from the pros on what experience on the range has taught them. Competitive events are going on all the time with rifles, pistols, and shotguns. You can find trap and skeet shoots, pistol matches emphasizing gun-handling skills, long-range rifle matches, and even pellet and BB gun competitions.

It may take a while before you have a crack at The Gunny's favorite, the National Rifle Matches at Camp Perry, but after you show up there on your own or with a team, you'll find yourself marking the event with red letters on your calendar every year.

I look forward to every rifle match I attend like a kid waiting for Christmas. From the minute I arrive on the range and start seeing old friends, I start feeling like a kid again. The atmosphere is energizing.

> **I look forward to every rifle match I attend like a kid waiting for Christmas.**

You see, I've had this love affair with the M1 Garand since the first time I picked one up and shot it, back in recruit training in 1961. These were M1s used by all the recruits. You could shake 'em and they would rattle. These guns were flat worn out, but you could still take 'em out on the rifle range and shoot high expert with them. Which, I'm proud to say, I did.

When John C. Garand built this weapon, he built it to withstand anything. You can throw it into the mud, abuse it, then pick it up and it will shoot six hundred yards. You can buy match-quality barrels to go on this rifle if you want, but mine is right off the rack, and I chew up the center of the target at six hundred yards all day long.

These are great rifles, with hardly ever a malfunction. If there is a malfunction, it's usually the ammo. The Garand fires a .30-06 round, which will kill anything you hunt in North America. That's my favorite hunting load, depending, of course, on what we're hunting. As far as I'm concerned a .30-06 is the best all-around hunting rifle to use in North America.

My second favorite is the M1A, which is the M14 dressed down for civilians. It's gas-operated, has a wood stock and iron sights, and it fires a .308 caliber round. My third favorite is the bolt-action

Springfield '03, which our troops used in World War I. It fires a .30-06 like the M1 and is one of the most accurate rifles in history. Those are the three guns I compete with. The ammo I use is loaded by Creedmoor Sports in Anniston, Alabama, a company run by my good friend and shooting partner, Dennis DeMille (www.creedmoorsports. com).

Creedmoor uses the best components money can buy in their .30-06 load. In the summer of 2014, they will begin selling directly to the public and through the Civilian Marksmanship Program. It's all-around great ammo.

A few years ago I made a move toward modern technology while shooting with my team at Camp Perry and promptly fell on my ass. I had ordered a custom AR-15 Black Gun, match-conditioned, the whole ball of wax. But as soon as I walked off the six-hundred-yard line there at Camp Perry, I had had about as much of the AR as I could take. As I left my firing point, I announced, "This damn gun is for sale!" And I sold it right there, before I even left the range, for $1,800, exactly the amount I had paid for it.

That was the second match I had shot with the AR-15. I gave it two matches to show me what it could do. It seemed so different from the M1 Garand and the M14 and the '03—the rifles I usually shoot. The AR is so totally different, starting with its pistol grip. With the other rifles, you hold the small of the stock and pull straight back on your shoulder. With the AR, you hang on to that pistol grip, and what happens is that when you get a little heavy on that trigger, you pull the rifle right or left. With the '03, the M1, and the M14, you pull it back into your shoulder more. Anytime you see me on the rifle range now, you can expect to see me shouldering an M1, '03, or M14. If it ain't got wood on it, you won't see me shooting it.

Our team recently introduced a new tool into our practice shooting that has helped improve our scores—mine in particular.

The offhand position was eating my lunch. There was a certain amount of meditation and talking to myself going on when I stepped up to the two-hundred-yard line to take the offhand position. But I just couldn't find any sure cures for my unsteady hands. I'd had coaching and had tried everything in the book.

Then our team started practicing with an air rifle that looks exactly like an M16. This rifle, called the National Match Air Rifle (NMAR), was another invention of my friend Dennis at Creedmoor Sports. He designed and had machined a stock kit that wrapped around one of the world's most accurate air rifles, the German Anschutz 8001. It was a thing of beauty. Unfortunately, it was so expensive to make that they only made about two hundred before shutting down production. In the world of high-end air rifles, it was relatively inexpensive for what it was, but high-power rifle shooters just couldn't bring themselves to fork over as much for an air rifle as they do for a "real" rifle. I'm lucky enough to own two of these rifles. For me it was just what I needed to improve my scores. (I still don't have any use for the AR.)

Another new development in our rifle matches is participation in relatively new sniper shooting matches. The popularity of sniper matches is soaring, and they have been added to both the Creedmoor and the National Matches at Camp Perry.

In vintage sniper rifle matches, you can shoot any rifle that is designated a pre-1952 sniper rifle. I shoot the M1 Garand D model while my shooting partner, Dennis, shoots the '03A4 Springfield. One rifle and its scope are set up for three hundred yards, the other for six hundred. We alternate, each guy shooting both ranges and both rifles. Talk about fun!

Like many veterans I still love to shoot, and I still love competition. I only wish my calendar were marked with more days spent on the range.

YOUNG MARINES DESERVE OUR SUPPORT

You can't be more Gunny Approved™ than the Young Marines of the Marine Corps League (www.youngmarines.com), to which I have given my support in fund-raising appearances and promotional testimonials since 2004. Dedicated to strengthening the lives of America's youth, the organization has Young Marines (aged eight through eighteen) participate in physical activities, survival training, and the personal development of core values in leadership, discipline, and teamwork. At present, the organization has over three hundred units with more than thirteen thousand Young Marines and three thousand adult volunteers, with affiliates in many foreign countries, including Germany and Japan.

THE GUNNY AND GLOCK: PARTNERS WITH A PURPOSE

After ten years of countless personal appearances and a string of internet videos that have been watched by literally millions, my association with GLOCK pistols is well known.

I like that. I like being GLOCK's spokesman. I like telling folks about a product I'm proud to back to the hilt. Where I once could ream out recruits at boot camp for three hours—without ever repeating myself—I now feel I could do the same three-hour run about the advantages of having a GLOCK in my hand.

I won't try to do that here, but I'll say this: GLOCK is the handgun of choice for approximately 70 percent of U.S. law enforcement agencies and the pistol of choice for a huge portion of military and law enforcement agencies throughout the world. With GLOCK, you have a solid head start on finding the pistol that's just right for your needs—home and personal defense, target shooting, or backcountry survival carry. My personal favorite to fill all those needs is the GLOCK 9 mm for target shooting, the 10 mm for hunting wild boars, and the .45 GAP for just about everything else.

The full-size Model 37 .45 GAP is just right for my particular grip, and, like all GLOCKs, it excels in accuracy and dependability. You can freeze it, leave it in the mud for days, and otherwise treat it in ways no Marine or soldier would ever think of, and yet the GLOCK will come out shooting. Its safety features are second to none, and it fills my hand as if it were custom-made for me.

I rely on GLOCKs for my home and personal protection. I hope I never have to use one for those purposes, but I assure you that if someone invades my high-desert property when I'm around, it's going to be their final mission.

I am extremely pleased with the recognition and many awards we've received from industry groups, such as The Telly Awards and The Communicator Awards, for GLOCK videos I've done. My manager, Bill Rogin, hates taking credit for his work. However, he wrote, produced, and directed each one of the "Somebody picked the wrong…" spots, and it's his genius that is all over the humorous yet dramatic scenarios showing GLOCKs in action against the bad guys.

To see these award-winning commercial videos, as well as others featuring straight talk about why I was a GLOCK owner even before I became the company spokesperson, go to YouTube and search for

"Gunny and GLOCK." Or you can always go to GLOCK's YouTube channel.

Those are just some of the gear, products, and companies that I've learned to respect and that I think you'll like too as you practice the art of getting squared away. When I discover a great product, I like to share it with my friends.

And you are my friends.

AFTERWORD

CLOSING THOUGHTS FROM MY MARINE

A Marine lives inside my head. Sometimes he talks to me.

My Marine tells me what it was like at Belleau Wood in World War I, when the German soldiers named him and his brothers "Devil Dogs." I cringe when he tells me about wading two hundred yards through a storm of machine-gun fire off the beach at Tarawa, where the landing crafts caught the wrong tide and dropped the troops offshore. When My Marine tells me about crawling up the lava dunes at Iwo Jima, the scene is more vivid than any I've known, because I've been there, my own boots in the sands that were once soaked with Marine blood. Sometimes My Marine reminds me about the icy retreat from the Chosin Reservoir in Korea, where he, outnumbered by tens of thousands of Chinese, fought his way out of the trap with frozen feet, bringing out his wounded and dead. Every man came back. No Marine was left behind. When My Marine tells me about Vietnam, I feel a flush of pride, because that was *my* war. I was there, serving alongside him.

The word Iraq brings forth a stream of remembrances from My Marine: battling the insurgents door-to-door in cities like Fallujah; learning to cope with the deadly ambushes of IEDs; the constant vigilance for suicide bombers so brain-dead they have no respect for their own lives or their fellow countrymen; firefights in the desert and hills with enemies who could appear to be friendly citizens one minute, then become attackers with automatic weapons and RPGs the next.

My Marine's voice is strong and emphatic when he describes the fighting in Afghanistan, where our forces put Taliban units on the run out of Kabul and the surrounding area, then spent years fighting both in the mountains and in the hot, dusty, and deadly provinces like Helmand. In Helmand, Taliban forces could make strikes on our troops, then retreat to refuges along the Pakistani border. In Afghanistan's tortuous, virtually roadless mountain terrain, ambushes were possible at every turn in the trail, from every ridge. My Marine says his units took the fight to the enemy, probing into the ranges, making the Taliban fight or flee. Whenever and wherever the Taliban chose to fight, they died.

My Marine tells me that right now there is no enemy of the United States he is not ready to face, no task or state of weariness that cannot be overcome with leg-pumping, back-humping, knuckle-busting effort. My Marine says he and his unit are squared away and motivated to the max, ready for any mission.

Then My Marine's voice becomes a whisper: "Don't forget me and my brothers and sisters. Honor us with your memory. Others must follow in our steps. Pass it on. Pass the word."

I tell him he can count on me!

—R. Lee Ermey